AGE
OF
JUSTICE
Compendium

W. D. Palmer

AuthorHouse™
1663 Liberty Drive
Bloomington, IN 47403
www.authorhouse.com
Phone: 833-262-8899

This book is printed on acid-free paper.

ISBN: 978-1-6655-2678-4 (sc)
ISBN: 978-1-6655-2679-1 (e)

Print information available on the last page.

Published by AuthorHouse 08/19/2021

authorHOUSE

Walter D. Palmer Leadership School

Currently W. D. Palmer is the founder and director of the W. D. Palmer Foundation (est. 1955), a repository of information-gathering on racism in health, education, employment, housing, courts, prisons, higher education, military, government, politics, law, banking, insurance, etc.

He is also the founder of the Black People's University of Philadelphia (1955) Freedom School, which was the grassroots organizing and training center for grassroots community and political leadership in Philadelphia and nationally. These organizations were run as nonprofit unincorporated associations from 1955 until 1980, when the Palmer Foundation received its 501(c)(3) federal tax exemption status.

W. D. Palmer has also been a professor, teaching American Racism at the University of Pennsylvania since the 1960's and today he is a member of the Presidents Commission on 1619, the 400-year anniversary of African slavery in America.

Professor Palmer has been a social activist leading the fight against racial injustice for over seventy years in Philadelphia and around the nation. In 2018, Philadelphia honored him for the organizing work he did to reform the Philadelphia school system in 1967.

In 2020, Philadelphia honored him for 65 years of fighting for social justice throughout the country. In 1980, he led the fight for parental school choice which helped the Governor of Pennsylvania get a law passed in 1997, and in 2000 he created the Walter D. Palmer Leadership Charter School.

In 2005, he borrowed eleven million dollars to build a 55 thousand square-foot two story building on two acres of land in North Philadelphia, which was donated to the school by the City of Philadelphia, and because of the school's rapid growth, in 2010 he acquired the Saint Bartholomew Catholic High School, for his middle and high school.

In ten years, the school grew from three hundred elementary and middle school students, to two hundred preschoolers and over a thousand kindergarten to twelfth graders. In 2005,

W. D. Palmer commissioned a muralist to paint over four hundred pre-selected portraits on the school walls, corridors, and stairwells, with a goal to paint thirty fifteen foot murals in the gymnatorium.

Although the Walter D. Palmer Leadership School recruited "at risk children" that were from seventeen of the poorest zip codes in Philadelphia and 300 percent below poverty, the school boasted of a 95% daily attendance, 100% high school graduation, and 100% post graduate placement in four year and two year colleges, trade and technology schools, or military until the school's closing in 2015.

Property Of

Name: _____

Address: _____

_____

Phone: _____

Email: _____

Emergency Contact: _____

Acknowledgement

I would like to take this time to acknowledge from the beginning of the Palmer Foundation, 1955, the many contributors who helped to gather information, organize, and write the leadership, self-development, and social awareness curriculums.

From the Palmer Foundation's inception, these contributors have been composed of community members, elementary, middle- and high-school students, as well as college student volunteers and interns, along with professional contributors.

We chose this method and process because it was consistent with our history, vision, philosophy, mission, and goals of always developing leadership in practice.

These groups, who have helped to produce our materials, are the same cohorts who over the years have helped to teach and train others as well as helped to develop a national database through which these curriculum and training materials can be distributed.

The story of the Palmer Foundation is the story of building community and leadership at the same time, and the Palmer Foundation wants to give an enthusiastic endorsement in recognition of the thousands of people who have been with us on this long and arduous journey.

We want to take this time to thank the many community leaders and people that have invited us into their communities to help them reclaim and restore the many values, properties, and people who may have been threatened with the loss of finance, property, and life, because they are the true heroes and heroines that made the Palmer Foundation the success that it has become.

Public Appeal

The Palmer Foundation is a federal 501(c)(3) organization that has spent over 65 years educating and fighting for social justice in the most underserved "at risk" communities around the country. Our goals have always been to use education for human liberation and encourage "at risk" families and children to help gather, write, produce, publish, and teach others in a similar situation.

Our mission is to disseminate our leadership, self-development, social justice, and grassroots-organizing books, manuals, and learning materials across America and around the world.

Our goals are to sell these publications or to offer them in exchange for a suggested tax-exempt donation that would allow us to continue producing our leadership training, as well as grassroots community and political organizing efforts.

Ultimately, we would like to create a satellite school as a model or prototype of the Walter D. Palmer Leadership School that could be replicated around the world.

Volume 1 Table of Contents

INTRODUCTION

DR. PALMER, DISTINGUISHED PROFESSOR AND LIFELONG SOCIAL CHANGE ACTIVIST, ONE DAY ENCOUNTERS A MYSTERIOUS MAN WHO SAYS HIS NAME IS *MR. JAMES*...

AFTER BEFRIENDING DR. PALMER, MR. JAMES MYSTERIOUSLY DISAPPEARS. BUT BEFORE HE DOES, HE LEAVES DR. PALMER HIS FAVORITE WATCH.

AS DR. PALMER DISCOVERS, THE WATCH CONTAINS A HIDDEN *POWER DIAL*, WHICH ALLOWS HIM TO TRANSFORM FROM A 75-YEAR-OLD PROFESSOR INTO A REPLICA OF HIMSELF AT AGES 20, 30, 40, AND 50 – AT DIFFERENT STAGES OF HIS STRUGGLE FOR SOCIAL CHANGE.

I AM MR. JAMES. ALTHOUGH DR. PALMER DOES NOT KNOW IT YET, MYSELF AND OTHER EXTRA-CELESTIAL *AGENTS OF AGE* HAVE BEEN OBSERVING HIS LIFELONG STRUGGLE FOR SOCIAL CHANGE. WE WANT TO SUPPORT HIS EFFORTS.

DR. PALMER RECEIVES INSTRUCTIONS THAT HE MUST RETURN THE POWER DIAL IN NO MORE THAN 25 YEARS, WHEN HE REACHES AGE 100.

IN THE MEANTIME, HE HAS FULL USE OF THE POWER DIAL'S ABILITIES, AS WELL AS A RANGE OF OTHER DEVICES AND THE HELP OF SEVERAL SUPERNATURAL CREATURES, TO AID HIM IN HIS FIGHT FOR SOCIAL CHANGE.

TOPIC DEFINITION

EACH OF THE FOLLOWING PAGES IS FOCUSED ON A PARTICULAR SOCIETAL ISSUE.

EVERY TOPIC HAS A DEFINITION, INTENDED TO PROVIDE AN OVERVIEW AND BASIC FACTS AND STATISTICS.

THE GOAL OF THESE DEFINITIONS IS TO ENCOURAGE STUDENTS TO THINK ABOUT THE ISSUES AND TO PURSUE FURTHER RESEARCH AND LEARNING.

ULTIMATELY, WE WANT YOUNG PEOPLE TO THINK CREATIVELY AND FOR THEMSELVES ABOUT HOW TO RESPOND TO THESE ISSUES.

WHERE TO TURN?

EACH OF THE FOLLOWING PAGES CONTAINS A FORM WITH THE TITLE "WHERE TO TURN?" AND BLANK SPACES FOR CONTACT INFORMATION AT CITY, STATE, COUNTY, AND NATIONAL LEVELS.

STUDENTS ARE ENCOURAGED TO RESEARCH AND FILL OUT THESE FORMS, WITH THE HELP OF THEIR PARENTS AND TEACHERS. IN THIS WAY, STUDENTS, PARENTS, AND TEACHERS WILL EDUCATE THEMSELVES AND EACH OTHER WHILE GETTING INVOLVED IN THE PROJECT.

AFTER FILLING OUT THE "WHERE TO TURN" INFORMATION ON EACH PAGE, STUDENTS WILL HAVE PERSONALIZED BOOKLETS WITH THEIR OWN THINKING AND RESEARCH INSIDE.

ALCOHOL ABUSE

DR. PALMER, DISTINGUISHED PROFESSOR AND LIFELONG SOCIAL CHANGE ACTIVIST, ENCOUNTERS A MYSTERIOUS MAN CALLED MR. JAMES. UNKNOWN TO DR. PALMER, MR. JAMES IS AN *AGENT OF AGE*. PRIOR TO HIS DISAPPEARANCE, MR. JAMES LEAVES DR. PALMER HIS WRISTWATCH.

THE WATCH, DR. PALMER DISCOVERS, CONTAINS A HIDDEN *POWER DIAL*, WHICH WILL ALLOW HIM TO TRANSFORM FROM A 75-YEAR-OLD PROFESSOR INTO A REPLICA OF HIMSELF AT AGES 20, 30, 40, AND 50. THE WATCH, ALONG WITH A RANGE OF OTHER DEVICES AND THE HELP OF SEVERAL SUPERNATURAL CREATURES, ARE MEANT TO AID HIM IN HIS FIGHT FOR SOCIAL CHANGE.

AT AGE 20, DR. PALMER WAS AN *URBAN SURVIVALIST*, AN EXPERT AT NAVIGATING IN A TOUGH ENVIRONMENT AND LOOKING OUT FOR THOSE AROUND HIM.

NOW, HE USES THE POWER DIAL TO TRANFORM INTO HIS 20-YEAR-OLD SELF TO CONTINUE FIGHTING THE CHALLENGES HE CONFRONTED THEN.

POWER DIALS ARE THE SOURCE OF AN AGENT OF AGE'S ABILITIES. THEY ACT AS LINKS TO THE *GREATNESS OF TIME*.

DR. PALMER'S POWER DIAL ENABLES HIM TO *TRAVEL THROUGH TIME*. IT ALSO TELLS TIME ANYWHERE IN THE WORLD AND PROVIDES STATS ON ANY LOCAL ENVIRONMENT.

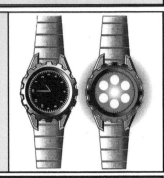

WHERE TO TURN?

WHERE SHOULD A YOUNG PERSON FACED WITH THIS ISSUE TURN? RESEARCH AND FILL OUT THE CONTACT INFORMATION BELOW.

IN YOUR CITY...

NAME: _____

PHONE: _____

EMAIL: _____

IN YOUR STATE...

NAME: _____

PHONE: _____

EMAIL: _____

IN YOUR COUNTY...

NAME: _____

PHONE: _____

EMAIL: _____

NATION-WIDE...

NAME: _____

PHONE: _____

EMAIL: _____

ALCOHOL ABUSE

IN THE U.S., NEARLY 17 MILLION ADULTS AGED 18 AND OLDER HAVE AN ALCOHOL ABUSE DISORDER.[1] IN ADDITION, MORE THAN 7 MILLION CHILDREN LIVE IN HOUSEHOLDS WITH AT LEAST ONE PARENT WHO DRINKS TOO MUCH.[2] *ALCOHOL ABUSE* IS DEFINED AS DRINKING IN EXCESS TO THE POINT WHERE IT CAUSES THE BODY HARM AND INTERFERES WITH LIVING A HEALTHY LIFE.

ALCOHOL IS ALSO A LEADING CAUSE OF DEATH. IN THE U.S., NEARLY 88,000 PEOPLE DIE ANNUALLY FROM ALCOHOL-RELATED CAUSES (IT'S RESPONSIBLE FOR NEARLY ONE THIRD OF DRIVING FATALITIES), MAKING IT THE THIRD LEADING PREVENTABLE CAUSE OF DEATH.[3]

ANIMAL ABUSE

DR. PALMER, DISTINGUISHED PROFESSOR AND LIFELONG SOCIAL CHANGE ACTIVIST, ENCOUNTERS A MYSTERIOUS MAN CALLED MR. JAMES. UNKNOWN TO DR. PALMER, MR. JAMES IS AN *AGENT OF AGE*. PRIOR TO HIS DISAPPEARANCE, MR. JAMES LEAVES DR. PALMER HIS WRISTWATCH.

THE WATCH, DR. PALMER DISCOVERS, CONTAINS A HIDDEN *POWER DIAL*, WHICH WILL ALLOW HIM TO TRANSFORM FROM A 75-YEAR-OLD PROFESSOR INTO A REPLICA OF HIMSELF AT AGES 20, 30, 40, AND 50. THE WATCH, ALONG WITH A RANGE OF OTHER DEVICES AND THE HELP OF SEVERAL SUPERNATURAL CREATURES, ARE MEANT TO AID HIM IN HIS FIGHT FOR SOCIAL CHANGE.

AT AGE 30, DR. PALMER WAS A *BLACK POWER ACTIVIST*, WORKING LOCALLY AND NATIONALLY TO DEMAND JUSTICE.

NOW, HE USES THE POWER DIAL TO TRANSFORM INTO HIS 30-YEAR-OLD SELF SO THAT HE CAN CONTINUE FIGHTING RACISM, DISCRIMINATION, AND HATE CRIMES.

ONE OF DR. PALMER'S DEVICES IS A PAIR OF *POWER SUNGLASSES*, WHICH PROVIDE HIM WITH DISTANT DAY AND NIGHT VISION AND ALLOW HIM TO SEE THROUGH DARKNESS, WALLS, RAIN, SNOW, AND DUST STORMS!

WHERE TO TURN?

WHERE SHOULD A YOUNG PERSON FACED WITH THIS ISSUE TURN? RESEARCH AND FILL OUT THE CONTACT INFORMATION BELOW.

IN YOUR CITY...

NAME: _____

PHONE: _____

EMAIL: _____

IN YOUR STATE...

NAME: _____

PHONE: _____

EMAIL: _____

IN YOUR COUNTY...

NAME: _____

PHONE: _____

EMAIL: _____

NATION-WIDE...

NAME: _____

PHONE: _____

EMAIL: _____

ANIMAL ABUSE

ANIMAL ABUSE COULD BE DELIBERATE HARM DIRECTED TOWARDS AN ANIMAL OR DEPRIVATION OF FOOD, WATER, OR SHELTER.

ANIMAL ABUSE IS VERY COMMON. IN FACT, EVERY YEAR, MORE THAN 10 MILLION ANIMALS DIE FROM ABUSE IN THE U.S. ALONE.[4]

COMMON TYPES OF ANIMAL ABUSE INCLUDE ABUSE OF PETS, ABUSE OF LIVESTOCK AND POULTRY FOR COMMERCIAL MOTIVES, AND PRACTICES SUCH AS DOGFIGHTING AND BULLFIGHTING.

IN ADDITION, INTENTIONAL CRUELTY TO ANIMALS IS STRONGLY CORRELATED WITH OTHER CRIMES, INCLUDING VIOLENCE AGAINST PEOPLE.[5]

ASBESTOS

DR. PALMER, DISTINGUISHED PROFESSOR AND LIFELONG SOCIAL CHANGE ACTIVIST, ENCOUNTERS A MYSTERIOUS MAN CALLED MR. JAMES. UNKNOWN TO DR. PALMER, MR. JAMES IS AN *AGENT OF AGE*. PRIOR TO HIS DISAPPEARANCE, MR. JAMES LEAVES DR. PALMER HIS WRISTWATCH.

THE WATCH, DR. PALMER DISCOVERS, CONTAINS A HIDDEN *POWER DIAL*, WHICH WILL ALLOW HIM TO TRANSFORM FROM A 75-YEAR-OLD PROFESSOR INTO A REPLICA OF HIMSELF AT AGES 20, 30, 40, AND 50. THE WATCH, ALONG WITH A RANGE OF OTHER DEVICES AND THE HELP OF SEVERAL SUPERNATURAL CREATURES, ARE MEANT TO AID HIM IN HIS FIGHT FOR SOCIAL CHANGE.

AT AGE 40, DR. PALMER WAS A *REVOLUTIONARY ACTIVIST*, TEACHING COMMUNITY ORGANIZING AND SUPPORTING MOVEMENTS FOR CHANGE NATIONALLY AND INTER-NATIONALLY.

NOW, HE CAN USE THE POWER DIAL TO TRANSFORM INTO HIS 40-YEAR-OLD SELF AND CONTINUE HIS WORK.

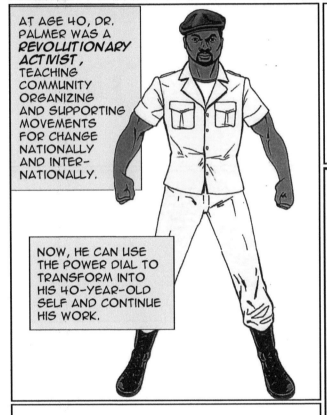

ONE OF DR. PALMER'S DEVICES IS A *POWER HEARING DEVICE*, WHICH CAN HEAR UP TO A MILE AWAY AND TRANSLATE ANY SPOKEN LANGUAGE INTO ENGLISH!

ASBESTOS

ASBESTOS IS A NATURAL MINERAL FIBER THAT CAN BE SPUN OR WOVEN SIMILARLY TO WOOL OR COTTON. IT IS FIRE-RESISTANT AND WAS A COMMONLY USED MATERIAL FOR MANY YEARS.

HOWEVER, AIRBORNE ASBESTOS FIBERS HAVE BEEN SHOWN TO CAUSE CANCER. ASBESTOS ALSO CAUSES A LUNG DISORDER CALLED *ASBESTOSIS.*

ALTHOUGH TODAY PEOPLE KNOW THAT ASBESTOS IS DANGEROUS, IT IS STILL PRESENT IN MANY BUILDINGS - INCLUDING HOMES AND SCHOOLS - THAT WERE BUILT BEFORE THE 1980S. IN ADDITION, MANY BUILDING MATERIALS THAT CONTAIN ASBESTOS ARE NOW DETERIORATING WITH AGE, CAUSING HIGHER RISK OF EXPOSURE.

WHERE TO TURN?

WHERE SHOULD A YOUNG PERSON FACED WITH THIS ISSUE TURN? RESEARCH AND FILL OUT THE CONTACT INFORMATION BELOW.

IN YOUR CITY...

NAME: _____

PHONE: _____

EMAIL: _____

IN YOUR STATE...

NAME: _____

PHONE: _____

EMAIL: _____

IN YOUR COUNTY...

NAME: _____

PHONE: _____

EMAIL: _____

NATION-WIDE...

NAME: _____

PHONE: _____

EMAIL: _____

BULLYING

DR. PALMER, DISTINGUISHED PROFESSOR AND LIFELONG SOCIAL CHANGE ACTIVIST, ENCOUNTERS A MYSTERIOUS MAN CALLED MR. JAMES. UNKNOWN TO DR. PALMER, MR. JAMES IS AN *AGENT OF AGE*. PRIOR TO HIS DISAPPEARANCE, MR. JAMES LEAVES DR. PALMER HIS WRISTWATCH.

THE WATCH, DR. PALMER DISCOVERS, CONTAINS A HIDDEN *POWER DIAL*, WHICH WILL ALLOW HIM TO TRANSFORM FROM A 75-YEAR-OLD PROFESSOR INTO A REPLICA OF HIMSELF AT AGES 20, 30, 40, AND 50. THE WATCH, ALONG WITH A RANGE OF OTHER DEVICES AND THE HELP OF SEVERAL SUPERNATURAL CREATURES, ARE MEANT TO AID HIM IN HIS FIGHT FOR SOCIAL CHANGE.

AT AGE 50, DR. PALMER WAS AN *ACADEMIC ACTIVIST*, ADVOCATING ON BEHALF OF STUDENTS AND TEACHING REAL-WORLD LEADERSHIP SKILLS.

NOW, HE CAN USE THE POWER DIAL TO TRANFORM INTO HIS 50-YEAR-OLD SELF AND CONTINUE THIS WORK.

AMONG DR. PALMER'S DEVICES IS A *POWER BICYCLE*, WHICH HAS 12 SPEEDS AND CAN CLIMB HILLS AND MOUNTAINS!

WHERE TO TURN?

WHERE SHOULD A YOUNG PERSON FACED WITH THIS ISSUE TURN? RESEARCH AND FILL OUT THE CONTACT INFORMATION BELOW.

IN YOUR CITY...

NAME: _____

PHONE: _____

EMAIL: _____

IN YOUR STATE...

NAME: _____

PHONE: _____

EMAIL: _____

IN YOUR COUNTY...

NAME: _____

PHONE: _____

EMAIL: _____

NATION-WIDE...

NAME: _____

PHONE: _____

EMAIL: _____

BULLYING

BULLYING IS PURPOSELY TORMENTING ANOTHER PERSON IN PHYSICAL, VERBAL, OR PSYCHOLOGICAL WAYS. IT CAN RANGE FROM HITTING, SHOVING, AND MOCKING TO DEMANDING MONEY OR POSSESSIONS.

IN THE U.S., 1 IN 5 STUDENTS AGED 12-18 HAS BEEN BULLIED IN SCHOOL,[6] AND 70% OF SCHOOL STAFF HAVE SEEN BULLYING.[7] IN ADDITION, THOUSANDS OF STUDENTS SKIP SCHOOL EACH YEAR BECAUSE THEY ARE BEING BULLIED.

COMMON TYPES OF BULLYING INCLUDE VERBAL HARASSMENT, SOCIAL HARASSMENT, PHYSICAL BULLYING, AND CYBERBULLYING.

CHILD ABUSE

DR. PALMER, DISTINGUISHED PROFESSOR AND LIFELONG SOCIAL CHANGE ACTIVIST, ENCOUNTERS A MYSTERIOUS MAN CALLED MR. JAMES. UNKNOWN TO DR. PALMER, MR. JAMES IS AN *AGENT OF AGE*. PRIOR TO HIS DISAPPEARANCE, MR. JAMES LEAVES DR. PALMER HIS WRISTWATCH.

THE WATCH, DR. PALMER DISCOVERS, CONTAINS A HIDDEN *POWER DIAL*, WHICH WILL ALLOW HIM TO TRANSFORM FROM A 75-YEAR-OLD PROFESSOR INTO A REPLICA OF HIMSELF AT AGES 20, 30, 40, AND 50. THE WATCH, ALONG WITH A RANGE OF OTHER DEVICES AND THE HELP OF SEVERAL SUPERNATURAL CREATURES, ARE MEANT TO AID HIM IN HIS FIGHT FOR SOCIAL CHANGE.

ONE OF DR. PALMER'S SUPERNATURAL ALLIES IS A GERMAN SHEPHERD GUARD DOG NAMED *WOLF*.

WOLF'S COLLAR CONTAINS A POWER DIAL SIMILAR TO THE ONE IN DR. PALMER'S WATCH. THE POWER DIAL GIVES WOLF SUPERNATURAL ABILITIES INCLUDING *IMMORTAL LIFE!*

AMONG DR. PALMER'S DEVICES IS A *POWER SONAR DEVICE*, WHICH ALLOWS HIM TO DETECT OBJECTS UNDERWATER!

CHILD ABUSE

CHILD ABUSE IS THE MALTREATMENT OF A CHILD BY A PARENT OR CARETAKER.

CHILD ABUSE IS VERY WIDESPREAD. IN FACT, IT IS ESTIMATED THAT 1 IN 7 CHILDREN IN THE U.S. HAS EXPERIENCED ABUSE AND/OR NEGLECT IN THE PAST YEAR.[8]

IN ADDITION, ADULT SURVIVORS OF CHILD ABUSE ARE MORE LIKELY TO EXPERIENCE MENTAL HEALTH DIFFICULTIES, INCLUDING DEPRESSION, ANXIETY, BIPOLAR DISORDER, PTSD, EATING DISORDERS, AND SUBSTANCE USE DISORDERS.[9]

CHILDREN WHO HAVE EXPERIENCED ABUSE OR NEGLECT ARE ALSO MORE LIKELY TO ENGAGE IN HIGH-RISK BEHAVIORS LIKE SMOKING, ALCOHOL AND DRUG USE, AND UNSAFE SEX.[10]

WHERE TO TURN?

WHERE SHOULD A YOUNG PERSON FACED WITH THIS ISSUE TURN? RESEARCH AND FILL OUT THE CONTACT INFORMATION BELOW.

IN YOUR CITY...
NAME: _____
PHONE: _____
EMAIL: _____

IN YOUR STATE...
NAME: _____
PHONE: _____
EMAIL: _____

IN YOUR COUNTY...
NAME: _____
PHONE: _____
EMAIL: _____

NATION-WIDE...
NAME: _____
PHONE: _____
EMAIL: _____

DISABILITY

DR. PALMER, DISTINGUISHED PROFESSOR AND LIFELONG SOCIAL CHANGE ACTIVIST, ENCOUNTERS A MYSTERIOUS MAN CALLED MR. JAMES. UNKNOWN TO DR. PALMER, MR. JAMES IS AN *AGENT OF AGE*. PRIOR TO HIS DISAPPEARANCE, MR. JAMES LEAVES DR. PALMER HIS WRISTWATCH.

THE WATCH, DR. PALMER DISCOVERS, CONTAINS A HIDDEN *POWER DIAL*, WHICH WILL ALLOW HIM TO TRANSFORM FROM A 75-YEAR-OLD PROFESSOR INTO A REPLICA OF HIMSELF AT AGES 20, 30, 40, AND 50. THE WATCH, ALONG WITH A RANGE OF OTHER DEVICES AND THE HELP OF SEVERAL SUPERNATURAL CREATURES, ARE MEANT TO AID HIM IN HIS FIGHT FOR SOCIAL CHANGE.

AMONG DR. PALMER'S SUPERNATURAL ALLIES ARE THE *GUARDIAN GODS* OF ALL SEVEN CONTINENTS.

NORTH AMERICA, THE *GUARDIAN OF WATER*, CAN CONTROL TIDES, BUILD GIANT WAVES, AND FLOOD RIVERS AND LAKES TO ASSIST DR. PALMER!

ONE OF DR. PALMER'S DEVICES IS A *POWER JET SKI*, WHICH CAN REACH 75-100 MPH AND CONVERT INTO A MOTORCYCLE ON LAND!

WHERE TO TURN?

WHERE SHOULD A YOUNG PERSON FACED WITH THIS ISSUE TURN? RESEARCH AND FILL OUT THE CONTACT INFORMATION BELOW.

IN YOUR CITY...

NAME: _____

PHONE: _____

EMAIL: _____

IN YOUR STATE...

NAME: _____

PHONE: _____

EMAIL: _____

IN YOUR COUNTY...

NAME: _____

PHONE: _____

EMAIL: _____

NATION-WIDE...

NAME: _____

PHONE: _____

EMAIL: _____

DISABILITY

AROUND THE WORLD, OVER 1 BILLION PEOPLE – 15% OF THE WORLD'S POPULATION – LIVE WITH SOME FORM OF *DISABILITY*.[11] IN THE U.S., 19% OF THE POPULATION HAS A DISABILITY, AND ABOUT 10% HAVE A SEVERE DISABILITY.[12]

IN SPITE OF HOW COMMON DISABILITIES ARE, PEOPLE LIVING WITH THEM FACE HIGHER RATES OF UNEMPLOYMENT, LOWER SALARIES, AND HIGHER RATES OF POVERTY THAN NON-DISABLED PEOPLE.[13] IN ADDITION, CHILDREN WITH DISABILITIES ARE LESS LIKELY TO ATTEND SCHOOL THAN NON-DISABLED CHILDREN.[14]

DISABILITY DISCRIMINATION

DR. PALMER, DISTINGUISHED PROFESSOR AND LIFELONG SOCIAL CHANGE ACTIVIST, ENCOUNTERS A MYSTERIOUS MAN CALLED MR. JAMES. UNKNOWN TO DR. PALMER, MR. JAMES IS AN *AGENT OF AGE*. PRIOR TO HIS DISAPPEARANCE, MR. JAMES LEAVES DR. PALMER HIS WRISTWATCH.

THE WATCH, DR. PALMER DISCOVERS, CONTAINS A HIDDEN *POWER DIAL*, WHICH WILL ALLOW HIM TO TRANSFORM FROM A 75-YEAR-OLD PROFESSOR INTO A REPLICA OF HIMSELF AT AGES 20, 30, 40, AND 50. THE WATCH, ALONG WITH A RANGE OF OTHER DEVICES AND THE HELP OF SEVERAL SUPERNATURAL CREATURES, ARE MEANT TO AID HIM IN HIS FIGHT FOR SOCIAL CHANGE.

AMONG DR. PALMER'S SUPERNATURAL ALLIES ARE THE *GUARDIAN GODS* OF ALL SEVEN CONTINENTS.

SOUTH AMERICA, THE *GUARDIAN OF FIRE*, CAN AID DR. PAMER BY CREATING WALLS OF FIRE AS A BLOCKADE AGAINST EVIL FORCES AND BY USING SMOKE AS A COVER OR DETERRENT FOR HIM!

ONE OF DR. PALMER'S DEVICES IS A *POWER HELICOPTER* THAT CAN REACH SPEEDS OF UP TO 400 MPH!

WHERE TO TURN?

WHERE SHOULD A YOUNG PERSON FACED WITH THIS ISSUE TURN? RESEARCH AND FILL OUT THE CONTACT INFORMATION BELOW.

IN YOUR CITY...

NAME: _____

PHONE: _____

EMAIL: _____

IN YOUR STATE...

NAME: _____

PHONE: _____

EMAIL: _____

IN YOUR COUNTY...

NAME: _____

PHONE: _____

EMAIL: _____

NATION-WIDE...

NAME: _____

PHONE: _____

EMAIL: _____

DISABILITY DISCRIMINATION

DISABILITY DISCRIMINATION, OR *ABLEISM*, IS THE UNEQUAL TREATMENT OF PEOPLE WITH DISABILITIES.

IN 1990, THE *AMERICANS WITH DISABILITIES ACT* WAS PASSED TO PROTECT PEOPLE WITH DISABILITIES FROM DISCRIMINATION IN JOBS.

HOWEVER, DISABLED PEOPLE STILL REPORT HIRING DISCRIMINATION AND WORKPLACE DISCRIMINATION.[15] IN ADDITION, THEY STILL FACE HIGHER UNEMPLOYMENT RATES, HIGHER POVERTY RATES, AND RECEIVE LOWER SALARIES THAN NON-DISABLED PEOPLE.[16]

DOMESTIC ABUSE

DR. PALMER, DISTINGUISHED PROFESSOR AND LIFELONG SOCIAL CHANGE ACTIVIST, ENCOUNTERS A MYSTERIOUS MAN CALLED MR. JAMES. UNKNOWN TO DR. PALMER, MR. JAMES IS AN *AGENT OF AGE*. PRIOR TO HIS DISAPPEARANCE, MR. JAMES LEAVES DR. PALMER HIS WRISTWATCH.

THE WATCH, DR. PALMER DISCOVERS, CONTAINS A HIDDEN *POWER DIAL*, WHICH WILL ALLOW HIM TO TRANSFORM FROM A 75-YEAR-OLD PROFESSOR INTO A REPLICA OF HIMSELF AT AGES 20, 30, 40, AND 50. THE WATCH, ALONG WITH A RANGE OF OTHER DEVICES AND THE HELP OF SEVERAL SUPERNATURAL CREATURES, ARE MEANT TO AID HIM IN HIS FIGHT FOR SOCIAL CHANGE.

AMONG DR. PALMER'S SUPERNATURAL ALLIES ARE THE *GUARDIAN GODS* OF ALL SEVEN CONTINENTS.

ASIA, THE *GUARDIAN OF THE SUN*, CAN ASSIST DR. PALMER BY INCREASING THE SUN'S HEAT OR CAUSING TEMPORARY BLINDNESS TO OVERWHELM AN ADVERSARY!

ONE OF DR. PALMER'S DEVICES IS A *POWER JETPACK*, WHICH CAN REACH SPEEDS OF 50 MPH AND TRAVEL AT UP TO 4000 FT ABOVE LAND!

WHERE TO TURN?

WHERE SHOULD A YOUNG PERSON FACED WITH THIS ISSUE TURN? RESEARCH AND FILL OUT THE CONTACT INFORMATION BELOW.

IN YOUR CITY...

NAME: _____

PHONE: _____

EMAIL: _____

IN YOUR STATE...

NAME: _____

PHONE: _____

EMAIL: _____

IN YOUR COUNTY...

NAME: _____

PHONE: _____

EMAIL: _____

NATION-WIDE...

NAME: _____

PHONE: _____

EMAIL: _____

DOMESTIC ABUSE

DOMESTIC ABUSE IS PHYSICAL, EMOTIONAL, OR SEXUAL VIOLENCE AGAINST A SPOUSE OR PARTNER.

DOMESTIC ABUSE IS VERY COMMON – IN FACT, 1 IN 4 WOMEN AND 1 IN 9 MEN EXPERIENCE SOME FORM OF ABUSE FROM THEIR PARTNERS.[17] 1 IN 10 WOMEN HAVE BEEN RAPED BY THEIR PARTNERS.[18] IN ADDITION, DOMESTIC VIOLENCE ACCOUNTS FOR 15% OF ALL VIOLENT CRIME.[19]

DOMESTIC ABUSE ALSO HAS CONSEQUENCES THAT GO BEYOND IMMEDIATE PHYSICAL DANGER. FOR INSTANCE, PEOPLE WHO HAVE EXPERIENCED DOMESTIC VIOLENCE HAVE HIGHER RATES OF DEPRESSION AND SUICIDAL BEHAVIOR THAN THOSE WHO HAVEN'T.[20]

DRUG ABUSE

DR. PALMER, DISTINGUISHED PROFESSOR AND LIFELONG SOCIAL CHANGE ACTIVIST, ENCOUNTERS A MYSTERIOUS MAN CALLED MR. JAMES. UNKNOWN TO DR. PALMER, MR. JAMES IS AN *AGENT OF AGE.* PRIOR TO HIS DISAPPEARANCE, MR. JAMES LEAVES DR. PALMER HIS WRISTWATCH.

THE WATCH, DR. PALMER DISCOVERS, CONTAINS A HIDDEN *POWER DIAL,* WHICH WILL ALLOW HIM TO TRANSFORM FROM A 75-YEAR-OLD PROFESSOR INTO A REPLICA OF HIMSELF AT AGES 20, 30, 40, AND 50. THE WATCH, ALONG WITH A RANGE OF OTHER DEVICES AND THE HELP OF SEVERAL SUPERNATURAL CREATURES, ARE MEANT TO AID HIM IN HIS FIGHT FOR SOCIAL CHANGE.

AMONG DR. PALMER'S SUPERNATURAL ALLIES ARE THE *GUARDIAN GODS* OF ALL SEVEN CONTINENTS.

AUSTRALIA, THE *GUARDIAN OF THE MOON,* CAN HAVE THE MOON RETREAT TO CAUSE DARKNESS, CONFUSION, AND A COVER FOR DR. PALMER!

ONE OF DR. PALMER'S DEVICES IS A *POWER RADAR DEVICE,* WHICH PROVIDES HIM WITH AIR SURVEILLANCE!

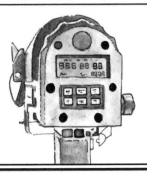

DRUG ABUSE

DRUG ABUSE IS THE USE OF ADDICTIVE DRUGS IN A WAY THAT LEADS TO INCREASED RISK OF HARM AND INABILITY TO CONTROL USE. SOME OF THE MOST COMMON CATEGORIES OF DRUGS INCLUDE:

STIMULANTS, SUCH AS METH, COCAINE, AND CRACK COCAINE, WHICH SPEED UP YOUR BODY TO MAKE YOU FEEL HIGH AND ENERGIZED.

DEPRESSANTS, SUCH AS XANAX, KLONOPIN, AND BARBITURATES, WHICH SLOW YOUR BODY DOWN.

OPIOIDS, SUCH AS OPIUM, MORPHINE, HEROIN, AND FENTANYL, WHICH RELIEVE PAIN.

HALLUCINOGENS, SUCH AS LSD AND ECSTASY/MDMA, WHICH AFFECT YOUR MOOD AND CAN MAKE YOU SEE OR HEAR THINGS THAT AREN'T REALLY THERE.

WHERE TO TURN?

WHERE SHOULD A YOUNG PERSON FACED WITH THIS ISSUE TURN? RESEARCH AND FILL OUT THE CONTACT INFORMATION BELOW.

IN YOUR CITY...

NAME: _____

PHONE: _____

EMAIL: _____

IN YOUR STATE...

NAME: _____

PHONE: _____

EMAIL: _____

IN YOUR COUNTY...

NAME: _____

PHONE: _____

EMAIL: _____

NATION-WIDE...

NAME: _____

PHONE: _____

EMAIL: _____

EDUCATION DISCRIMINATION

DR. PALMER, DISTINGUISHED PROFESSOR AND LIFELONG SOCIAL CHANGE ACTIVIST, ENCOUNTERS A MYSTERIOUS MAN CALLED MR. JAMES. UNKNOWN TO DR. PALMER, MR. JAMES IS AN *AGENT OF AGE*. PRIOR TO HIS DISAPPEARANCE, MR. JAMES LEAVES DR. PALMER HIS WRISTWATCH.

THE WATCH, DR. PALMER DISCOVERS, CONTAINS A HIDDEN *POWER DIAL*, WHICH WILL ALLOW HIM TO TRANSFORM FROM A 75-YEAR-OLD PROFESSOR INTO A REPLICA OF HIMSELF AT AGES 20, 30, 40, AND 50. THE WATCH, ALONG WITH A RANGE OF OTHER DEVICES AND THE HELP OF SEVERAL SUPERNATURAL CREATURES, ARE MEANT TO AID HIM IN HIS FIGHT FOR SOCIAL CHANGE.

AMONG DR. PALMER'S SUPERNATURAL ALLIES ARE THE *GUARDIAN GODS* OF ALL SEVEN CONTINENTS.

THE ARCTIC, *GUARDIAN OF WIND*, CAN REDIRECT WIND, STORMS, HURRICANES, AND CYCLONES TO ASSIST DR. PALMER!

ONE OF DR. PALMER'S DEVICES IS A *POWER SUBMARINE*, A HYPER-SUBMARINE THAT CAN REACH SPEEDS OF UP TO 50 MPH UNDERWATER!

WHERE TO TURN?

WHERE SHOULD A YOUNG PERSON FACED WITH THIS ISSUE TURN? RESEARCH AND FILL OUT THE CONTACT INFORMATION BELOW.

IN YOUR CITY...

NAME: _____

PHONE: _____

EMAIL: _____

IN YOUR STATE...

NAME: _____

PHONE: _____

EMAIL: _____

IN YOUR COUNTY...

NAME: _____

PHONE: _____

EMAIL: _____

NATION-WIDE...

NAME: _____

PHONE: _____

EMAIL: _____

EDUCATION DISCRIMINATION

EDUCATION DISCRIMINATION IS WHEN TEACHERS OR SCHOOL ADMINISTRATORS TREAT SOME STUDENTS UNFAIRLY COMPARED TO OTHERS.

DISCRIMINATION DUE TO RACE IS ESPECIALLY COMMON. FOR EXAMPLE, BLACK STUDENTS ARE 3.8 TIMES MORE LIKELY THAN WHITE STUDENTS TO RECEIVE ONE OR MORE SUSPENSIONS FROM SCHOOL.[91] STUDIES HAVE SHOWN THAT THIS IS BECAUSE BLACK STUDENTS ARE BEING PUNISHED AT A HIGHER RATE THAN OTHERS.[92]

BLACK STUDENTS ARE ALSO LESS LIKELY THAN WHITE STUDENTS TO BE SINGLED OUT IN POSITIVE WAYS. FOR INSTANCE, THEY ARE 54% LESS LIKELY TO BE RECOMMENDED FOR GIFTED-EDUCATION PROGRAMS, AFTER ADJUSTING FOR FACTORS SUCH AS STUDENTS' TEST SCORES.[93]

Volume 1 Citations

1. Hall, Kathleen. "10 Essential Facts About Alcohol Abuse." *Everydayhealth.com*. Accessed July 28, 2020, https://www.everydayhealth.com/news/essential-facts-about-alcohol-abuse/.
2. Hall, "Alcohol Abuse."
3. Hall, "Alcohol Abuse."
4. The Humane Society of the United States. "Animal cruelty facts and stats." Accessed July 21, 2020, https://www.humanesociety.org/resources/animal-cruelty-facts-and-stats.
5. Humane Society, "Animal Cruelty."
6. StopBullying.gov. "Facts About Bullying: Statistics." Accessed August 15, 2020, https://www.stopbullying.gov/media/facts/index.html.
7. National Center for Education Statistics, "Bullying: Fast Facts." Accessed august 15, 2020, https://nces.ed.gov/fastfacts/display.asp?id=719.
8. Centers for Disease Control and Prevention. "Child Abuse & Neglect: Fast Facts." Accessed August 15, 2020, https://www.cdc.gov/violenceprevention/childabuseandneglect/fastfact.html.
9. Springer, Kristen et al. "The Long-term Health Outcomes of Childhood Abuse." *Journal of General Internal Medicine*, October 18, 2003. Accessed August 15, 2020, https://www.ncbi.nlm.nih.gov/pmc/articles/PMC1494926/.
10. Springer et al., "Childhood Abuse."
11. World Health Organization. "10 facts on disability." Accessed August 9, 2020, https://www.who.int/features/factfiles/disability/en/.
12. World Health Organization, "10 facts on disability."
13. World Health Organization, "10 facts on disability."
14. World Health Organization, "10 facts on disability."
15. World Health Organization, "10 facts on disability."
16. World Health Organization, "10 facts on disability."
17. National Coalition Against Domestic Violence. "National Statistics." Accessed August 15, 2020, https://ncadv.org/statistics.
18. National Coalition Against Domestic Violence, "National Statistics."
19. National Coalition Against Domestic Violence, "National Statistics."
20. National Coalition Against Domestic Violence, "National Statistics."
21. Weir, Kirsten. "Inequality at school." *Apa.org*, accessed August 11, 2020, https://www.apa.org/monitor/2016/11/cover-inequality-school.
22. Weir, "Inequality at school."
23. Weir, "Inequality at school."

Chapter 2

Volume 2 Table of Contents

ELDER ABUSE

DR. PALMER, DISTINGUISHED PROFESSOR AND LIFELONG SOCIAL CHANGE ACTIVIST, ENCOUNTERS A MYSTERIOUS MAN CALLED MR. JAMES. UNKNOWN TO DR. PALMER, MR. JAMES IS AN *AGENT OF AGE*. PRIOR TO HIS DISAPPEARANCE, MR. JAMES LEAVES DR. PALMER HIS WRISTWATCH.

THE WATCH, DR. PALMER DISCOVERS, CONTAINS A HIDDEN *POWER DIAL*, WHICH WILL ALLOW HIM TO TRANSFORM FROM A 75-YEAR-OLD PROFESSOR INTO A REPLICA OF HIMSELF AT AGES 20, 30, 40, AND 50. THE WATCH, ALONG WITH A RANGE OF OTHER DEVICES AND THE HELP OF SEVERAL SUPERNATURAL CREATURES, ARE MEANT TO AID HIM IN HIS FIGHT FOR SOCIAL CHANGE.

AT AGE 20, DR. PALMER WAS AN *URBAN SURVIVALIST*, AN EXPERT AT NAVIGATING IN A TOUGH ENVIRONMENT AND LOOKING OUT FOR THOSE AROUND HIM.

NOW, HE USES THE POWER DIAL TO TRANSFORM INTO HIS 20-YEAR-OLD SELF TO CONTINUE FIGHTING THE CHALLENGES HE CONFRONTED THEN.

POWER DIALS ARE THE SOURCE OF AN AGENT OF AGE'S ABILITIES. THEY ACT AS LINKS TO THE *GREATNESS OF TIME*.

DR. PALMER'S POWER DIAL ENABLES HIM TO *TRAVEL THROUGH TIME*. IT ALSO TELLS TIME ANYWHERE IN THE WORLD AND PROVIDES STATS ON ANY LOCAL ENVIRONMENT.

WHERE TO TURN?

WHERE SHOULD A YOUNG PERSON FACED WITH THIS ISSUE TURN? RESEARCH AND FILL OUT THE CONTACT INFORMATION BELOW.

IN YOUR CITY...

NAME: _____

PHONE: _____

EMAIL: _____

IN YOUR STATE...

NAME: _____

PHONE: _____

EMAIL: _____

IN YOUR COUNTY...

NAME: _____

PHONE: _____

EMAIL: _____

NATION-WIDE...

NAME: _____

PHONE: _____

EMAIL: _____

ELDER ABUSE

ELDER ABUSE IS THE MISTREATMENT OR NEGLECT OF AN OLDER ADULT. COMMON FORMS OF ELDER ABUSE INCLUDE PHYSICAL ABUSE, FINANCIAL EXPLOITATION, EMOTIONAL ABUSE, AND DISCRIMINATION.

ELDER ABUSE IS VERY COMMON – IN THE U.S., APPROXOMATELY 1 IN 10 AMERICANS AGED 60+ HAVE EXPERIENCED SOME FORM OF ELDER ABUSE.[1] IN ADDITION, IN ALMOST 60% OF ELDER ABUSE AND NEGLECT INCIDENTS, THE PERPETRATOR IS A FAMILY MEMBER.[2]

ELDER ABUSE HAS SERIOUS CONSEQUENCES. FOR INSTANCE, OLDER ADULTS WHO HAVE BEEN ABUSED HAVE A 300% HIGHER RISK OF DEATH WITHIN THE NEXT 3 YEARS COMPARED WITH THOSE WHO HAVEN'T.[3]

EMPLOYMENT DISCRIMINATION

DR. PALMER, DISTINGUISHED PROFESSOR AND LIFELONG SOCIAL CHANGE ACTIVIST, ENCOUNTERS A MYSTERIOUS MAN CALLED MR. JAMES. UNKNOWN TO DR. PALMER, MR. JAMES IS AN *AGENT OF AGE*. PRIOR TO HIS DISAPPEARANCE, MR. JAMES LEAVES DR. PALMER HIS WRISTWATCH.

THE WATCH, DR. PALMER DISCOVERS, CONTAINS A HIDDEN *POWER DIAL*, WHICH WILL ALLOW HIM TO TRANSFORM FROM A 75-YEAR-OLD PROFESSOR INTO A REPLICA OF HIMSELF AT AGES 20, 30, 40, AND 50. THE WATCH, ALONG WITH A RANGE OF OTHER DEVICES AND THE HELP OF SEVERAL SUPERNATURAL CREATURES, ARE MEANT TO AID HIM IN HIS FIGHT FOR SOCIAL CHANGE.

AT AGE 30, DR. PALMER WAS A *BLACK POWER ACTIVIST*, WORKING LOCALLY AND NATIONALLY TO DEMAND JUSTICE.

NOW, HE USES THE POWER DIAL TO TRANFORM INTO HIS 30-YEAR-OLD SELF SO THAT HE CAN CONTINUE FIGHTING RACISM, DISCRIMINATION, AND HATE CRIMES.

ONE OF DR. PALMER'S DEVICES IS A PAIR OF *POWER SUNGLASSES*, WHICH PROVIDE HIM WITH DISTANT DAY AND NIGHT VISION AND ALLOW HIM TO SEE THROUGH DARKNESS, WALLS, RAIN, SNOW, AND DUST STORMS!

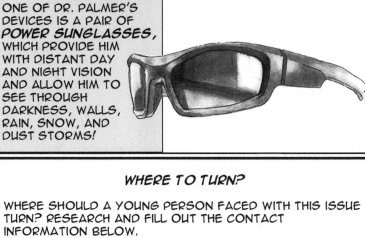

WHERE TO TURN?

WHERE SHOULD A YOUNG PERSON FACED WITH THIS ISSUE TURN? RESEARCH AND FILL OUT THE CONTACT INFORMATION BELOW.

IN YOUR CITY...

NAME: _____

PHONE: _____

EMAIL: _____

IN YOUR STATE...

NAME: _____

PHONE: _____

EMAIL: _____

IN YOUR COUNTY...

NAME: _____

PHONE: _____

EMAIL: _____

NATION-WIDE...

NAME: _____

PHONE: _____

EMAIL: _____

EMPLOYMENT DISCRIMINATION

EMPLOYMENT DISCRIMINATION IS WHEN PEOPLE ARE TREATED UNFAIRLY AT THEIR JOBS. COMMON TYPES OF DISCRIMINATION INCLUDE:

UNFAIR TREATMENT BASED ON RACE, RELIGION, AGE, GENDER, DISABILITY, OR SEXUAL ORIENTATION.

HARASSMENT BY MANAGERS OR CO-WORKERS.

DENIAL OF A REASONABLE WORKPLACE CHANGE NEEDED BECAUSE OF RELIGIOUS BELIEFS OR DISABILITY.

RETALIATION AGAINST COMPLAINTS MADE ABOUT DISCRIMINATION.

ENVIRONMENTAL ABUSE

DR. PALMER, DISTINGUISHED PROFESSOR AND LIFELONG SOCIAL CHANGE ACTIVIST, ENCOUNTERS A MYSTERIOUS MAN CALLED MR. JAMES. UNKNOWN TO DR. PALMER, MR. JAMES IS AN *AGENT OF AGE*. PRIOR TO HIS DISAPPEARANCE, MR. JAMES LEAVES DR. PALMER HIS WRISTWATCH.

THE WATCH, DR. PALMER DISCOVERS, CONTAINS A HIDDEN *POWER DIAL*, WHICH WILL ALLOW HIM TO TRANSFORM FROM A 75-YEAR-OLD PROFESSOR INTO A REPLICA OF HIMSELF AT AGES 20, 30, 40, AND 50. THE WATCH, ALONG WITH A RANGE OF OTHER DEVICES AND THE HELP OF SEVERAL SUPERNATURAL CREATURES, ARE MEANT TO AID HIM IN HIS FIGHT FOR SOCIAL CHANGE.

AT AGE 40, DR. PALMER WAS A *REVOLUTIONARY ACTIVIST*, TEACHING COMMUNITY ORGANIZING AND SUPPORTING MOVEMENTS FOR CHANGE NATIONALLY AND INTER-NATIONALLY.

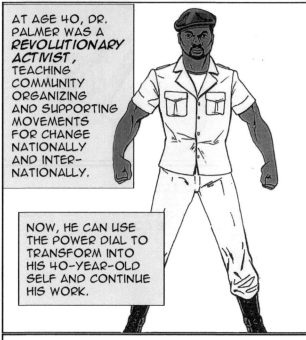

NOW, HE CAN USE THE POWER DIAL TO TRANSFORM INTO HIS 40-YEAR-OLD SELF AND CONTINUE HIS WORK.

ONE OF DR. PALMER'S DEVICES IS A *POWER HEARING DEVICE*, WHICH CAN HEAR UP TO A MILE AWAY AND TRANSLATE ANY SPOKEN LANGUAGE INTO ENGLISH!

WHERE TO TURN?

WHERE SHOULD A YOUNG PERSON FACED WITH THIS ISSUE TURN? RESEARCH AND FILL OUT THE CONTACT INFORMATION BELOW.

IN YOUR CITY...

NAME: _____

PHONE: _____

EMAIL: _____

IN YOUR STATE...

NAME: _____

PHONE: _____

EMAIL: _____

IN YOUR COUNTY...

NAME: _____

PHONE: _____

EMAIL: _____

NATION-WIDE...

NAME: _____

PHONE: _____

EMAIL: _____

ENVIRONMENTAL ABUSE

ENVIRONMENTAL ABUSE IS THE MISUSE OR OVERUSE OF EARTH'S NATURAL RESOURCES. SOME OF THE MOST IMPORTANT ENVIRONMENTAL ABUSE ISSUES ARE:

NATURAL RESOURCE USE: RECENT STUDIES HAVE SHOWN THAT HUMANITY USES SO MANY NATURAL RESOURCES THAT WE WOULD NEED ALMOST 1.5 EARTHS TO SUPPORT US.[4]

AIR POLLUTION: PARTICULARLY IN HEAVILY POPULATED CITIES, AIR POLLUTION IS BECOMING A DANGEROUS PROBLEM.

OVERFISHING: OVERFISHING LEADS TO A MISBALANCE OF OCEAN LIFE, SEVERELY AFFECTING NATURAL ECOSYSTEMS.

TRANSPORTATION: AN EVER-GROWING POPULATION NEEDS TRANSPORTATION, MUCH OF WHICH IS FUELED BY THE NATURAL RESOURCES THAT EMIT GREENHOUSE GASES, SUCH AS PETROLEUM.[5]

ETHNIC DISCRIMINATION

DR. PALMER, DISTINGUISHED PROFESSOR AND LIFELONG SOCIAL CHANGE ACTIVIST, ENCOUNTERS A MYSTERIOUS MAN CALLED MR. JAMES. UNKNOWN TO DR. PALMER, MR. JAMES IS AN *AGENT OF AGE*. PRIOR TO HIS DISAPPEARANCE, MR. JAMES LEAVES DR. PALMER HIS WRISTWATCH.

THE WATCH, DR. PALMER DISCOVERS, CONTAINS A HIDDEN *POWER DIAL*, WHICH WILL ALLOW HIM TO TRANSFORM FROM A 75-YEAR-OLD PROFESSOR INTO A REPLICA OF HIMSELF AT AGES 20, 30, 40, AND 50. THE WATCH, ALONG WITH A RANGE OF OTHER DEVICES AND THE HELP OF SEVERAL SUPERNATURAL CREATURES, ARE MEANT TO AID HIM IN HIS FIGHT FOR SOCIAL CHANGE.

AT AGE 50, DR. PALMER WAS AN *ACADEMIC ACTIVIST*, ADVOCATING ON BEHALF OF STUDENTS AND TEACHING REAL-WORLD LEADERSHIP SKILLS.

NOW, HE CAN USE THE POWER DIAL TO TRANFORM INTO HIS 50-YEAR-OLD SELF AND CONTINUE THIS WORK.

AMONG DR. PALMER'S DEVICES IS A *POWER BICYCLE*, WHICH HAS 12 SPEEDS AND CAN CLIMB HILLS AND MOUNTAINS!

WHERE TO TURN?

WHERE SHOULD A YOUNG PERSON FACED WITH THIS ISSUE TURN? RESEARCH AND FILL OUT THE CONTACT INFORMATION BELOW.

IN YOUR CITY...

NAME: _____

PHONE: _____

EMAIL: _____

IN YOUR STATE...

NAME: _____

PHONE: _____

EMAIL: _____

IN YOUR COUNTY...

NAME: _____

PHONE: _____

EMAIL: _____

NATION-WIDE...

NAME: _____

PHONE: _____

EMAIL: _____

ETHNIC DISCRIMINATION

ETHNIC DISCRIMINATION IS WHEN A PERSON IS TREATED UNFAIRLY BASED ON THEIR ETHNICITY.

ETHNICITY, AS OPPOSED TO RACE, IS OFTEN ASSOCIATED WITH CULTURAL EXPRESSION AND IDENTIFICATION RATHER THAN WITH PHYSICAL ATTRIBUTES. ETHNIC DISCRIMINATION IS OFTEN BASED ON A PERSON'S LANGUAGE OR CUSTOMS.

ETHNIC DISCRIMINATION OVERLAPS WITH OTHER FORMS OF DISCRIMINATION, SUCH AS EMPLOYMENT. FOR INSTANCE, IN ONE STUDY, 22% OF HISPANIC/LATINO WORKERS REPORTED EXPERIENCING WORKPLACE DISCRIMINATION, COMPARED TO ONLY 6% OF WHITE WORKERS.[6]

FIGHTING

DR. PALMER, DISTINGUISHED PROFESSOR AND LIFELONG SOCIAL CHANGE ACTIVIST, ENCOUNTERS A MYSTERIOUS MAN CALLED MR. JAMES. UNKNOWN TO DR. PALMER, MR. JAMES IS AN *AGENT OF AGE*. PRIOR TO HIS DISAPPEARANCE, MR. JAMES LEAVES DR. PALMER HIS WRISTWATCH.

THE WATCH, DR. PALMER DISCOVERS, CONTAINS A HIDDEN *POWER DIAL*, WHICH WILL ALLOW HIM TO TRANSFORM FROM A 75-YEAR-OLD PROFESSOR INTO A REPLICA OF HIMSELF AT AGES 20, 30, 40, AND 50. THE WATCH, ALONG WITH A RANGE OF OTHER DEVICES AND THE HELP OF SEVERAL SUPERNATURAL CREATURES, ARE MEANT TO AID HIM IN HIS FIGHT FOR SOCIAL CHANGE.

ONE OF DR. PALMER'S SUPERNATURAL ALLIES IS A GERMAN SHEPHERD GUARD DOG NAMED *WOLF*.

WOLF'S COLLAR CONTAINS A POWER DIAL SIMILAR TO THE ONE IN DR. PALMER'S WATCH. THE POWER DIAL GIVES WOLF SUPERNATURAL ABILITIES INCLUDING *IMMORTAL LIFE!*

AMONG DR. PALMER'S DEVICES IS A *POWER SONAR DEVICE*, WHICH ALLOWS HIM TO DETECT OBJECTS UNDERWATER!

WHERE TO TURN?

WHERE SHOULD A YOUNG PERSON FACED WITH THIS ISSUE TURN? RESEARCH AND FILL OUT THE CONTACT INFORMATION BELOW.

IN YOUR CITY...
- NAME: _____
- PHONE: _____
- EMAIL: _____

IN YOUR STATE...
- NAME: _____
- PHONE: _____
- EMAIL: _____

IN YOUR COUNTY...
- NAME: _____
- PHONE: _____
- EMAIL: _____

NATION-WIDE...
- NAME: _____
- PHONE: _____
- EMAIL: _____

FIGHTING

FIGHTING IS COMMON AMONG YOUNG PEOPLE, ESPECIALLY HIGH SCHOOL STUDENTS. IN FACT, IN 2017, ABOUT 1 IN 4 HIGH SCHOOL STUDENTS REPORTED BEING IN A PHYSICAL FIGHT IN THE PAST YEAR.[7]

THIS NUMBER VARIES BY GENDER AND RACE. MALE STUDENTS ARE MORE LIKELY TO REPORT BEING IN A FIGHT THAN FEMALE STUDENTS, AND NON-HISPANIC BLACK STUDENTS REPORT THE HIGHEST RATES OF BEING IN A FIGHT, FOLLOWED BY HISPANIC STUDENTS AND THEN NON-HISPANIC WHITE STUDENTS.[8]

IN ADDITION, MANY STUDENTS STAY HOME FROM SCHOOL BECAUSE THEY FEEL UNSAFE AT OR ON THEIR WAY TO OR FROM SCHOOL.[9]

FIRE SAFETY

DR. PALMER, DISTINGUISHED PROFESSOR AND LIFELONG SOCIAL CHANGE ACTIVIST, ENCOUNTERS A MYSTERIOUS MAN CALLED MR. JAMES. UNKNOWN TO DR. PALMER, MR. JAMES IS AN *AGENT OF AGE.* PRIOR TO HIS DISAPPEARANCE, MR. JAMES LEAVES DR. PALMER HIS WRISTWATCH.

THE WATCH, DR. PALMER DISCOVERS, CONTAINS A HIDDEN *POWER DIAL,* WHICH WILL ALLOW HIM TO TRANSFORM FROM A 75-YEAR-OLD PROFESSOR INTO A REPLICA OF HIMSELF AT AGES 20, 30, 40, AND 50. THE WATCH, ALONG WITH A RANGE OF OTHER DEVICES AND THE HELP OF SEVERAL SUPERNATURAL CREATURES, ARE MEANT TO AID HIM IN HIS FIGHT FOR SOCIAL CHANGE.

AMONG DR. PALMER'S SUPERNATURAL ALLIES ARE THE *GUARDIAN GODS* OF ALL SEVEN CONTINENTS.

SOUTH AMERICA, THE *GUARDIAN OF FIRE,* CAN AID DR. PAMER BY CREATING WALLS OF FIRE AS A BLOCKADE AGAINST EVIL FORCES AND BY USING SMOKE AS A COVER OR DETERRENT FOR HIM!

ONE OF DR. PALMER'S DEVICES IS A *POWER HELICOPTER* THAT CAN REACH SPEEDS OF UP TO 400 MPH!

WHERE TO TURN?

WHERE SHOULD A YOUNG PERSON FACED WITH THIS ISSUE TURN? RESEARCH AND FILL OUT THE CONTACT INFORMATION BELOW.

IN YOUR CITY...

NAME: _____

PHONE: _____

EMAIL: _____

IN YOUR STATE...

NAME: _____

PHONE: _____

EMAIL: _____

IN YOUR COUNTY...

NAME: _____

PHONE: _____

EMAIL: _____

NATION-WIDE...

NAME: _____

PHONE: _____

EMAIL: _____

FIRE SAFETY

FIRE SAFETY INVOLVES TAKING ACTION TO PREVENT FIRES FROM STARTING, SUCH AS INSTALLING WORKING SMOKE ALARMS, NOT LEAVING A STOVE UNATTENDED, AND KEEPING CLOSE WATCH OVER CANDLES.

FIRE SAFETY IS IMPORTANT. IN FACT, EVERY YEAR, MORE THAN 3,800 PEOPLE DIE FIRE-RELATED DEATHS IN THE U.S., AND AROUND 18,300 PEOPLE ARE INJURED IN FIRES.[10]

COMMON TYPES OF FIRES INCLUDE HOUSE FIRES, WHICH USUALLY START IN THE KITCHEN, AND FIRES IN COMMERCIAL BUILDINGS, WHICH ARE MOST COMMONLY DUE TO ARSON.

GAMBLING ABUSE

DR. PALMER, DISTINGUISHED PROFESSOR AND LIFELONG SOCIAL CHANGE ACTIVIST, ENCOUNTERS A MYSTERIOUS MAN CALLED MR. JAMES. UNKNOWN TO DR. PALMER, MR. JAMES IS AN *AGENT OF AGE*. PRIOR TO HIS DISAPPEARANCE, MR. JAMES LEAVES DR. PALMER HIS WRISTWATCH.

THE WATCH, DR. PALMER DISCOVERS, CONTAINS A HIDDEN *POWER DIAL*, WHICH WILL ALLOW HIM TO TRANSFORM FROM A 75-YEAR-OLD PROFESSOR INTO A REPLICA OF HIMSELF AT AGES 20, 30, 40, AND 50. THE WATCH, ALONG WITH A RANGE OF OTHER DEVICES AND THE HELP OF SEVERAL SUPERNATURAL CREATURES, ARE MEANT TO AID HIM IN HIS FIGHT FOR SOCIAL CHANGE.

AMONG DR. PALMER'S SUPERNATURAL ALLIES ARE THE *GUARDIAN GODS* OF ALL SEVEN CONTINENTS.

AFRICA, THE *GUARDIAN OF THE EARTH*, FIGHTS FOR PROTECTION OF THE ENVIRONMENT AND CAN AID DR. PALMER BY PROVIDING SHELTERS AND BLOCKADES OF EARTH!

ONE OF DR. PALMER'S DEVICES IS A *POWER MOTORCYCLE*, WHICH CAN REACH SPEEDS OF UP TO 150 MPH!

WHERE TO TURN?

WHERE SHOULD A YOUNG PERSON FACED WITH THIS ISSUE TURN? RESEARCH AND FILL OUT THE CONTACT INFORMATION BELOW.

IN YOUR CITY...

NAME: _____

PHONE: _____

EMAIL: _____

IN YOUR STATE...

NAME: _____

PHONE: _____

EMAIL: _____

IN YOUR COUNTY...

NAME: _____

PHONE: _____

EMAIL: _____

NATION-WIDE...

NAME: _____

PHONE: _____

EMAIL: _____

GAMBLING ABUSE

GAMBLING AFFECTS THE BRAIN'S REWARD SYSTEM SIMILARLY TO THE WAY DRUGS AND ALCOHOL DO, WHICH MEANS THAT GAMBLING CAN BECOME A SERIOUS ADDICTION.

IN FACT, GAMBLING IS CLOSELY LINKED WITH SUBSTANCE ABUSE. ONE STUDY FOUND THAT 75% OF GAMBLERS HAD AN ALCOHOL DISORDER, 38% HAD A DRUG USE DISORDER, AND 60% WERE NICOTINE DEPENDENT.[11]

GAMBLING IS ALSO LINKED TO MENTAL HEALTH DISORDERS. FOR INSTANCE, MANY GAMBLERS HAVE EXPERIENCED MENTAL HEALTH ISSUES SUCH AS MOOD DISORDERS, ANXIETY DISORDERS, AND PERSONALITY DISORDERS.[12]

GANGS

DR. PALMER, DISTINGUISHED PROFESSOR AND LIFELONG SOCIAL CHANGE ACTIVIST, ENCOUNTERS A MYSTERIOUS MAN CALLED MR. JAMES. UNKNOWN TO DR. PALMER, MR. JAMES IS AN *AGENT OF AGE*. PRIOR TO HIS DISAPPEARANCE, MR. JAMES LEAVES DR. PALMER HIS WRISTWATCH.

THE WATCH, DR. PALMER DISCOVERS, CONTAINS A HIDDEN *POWER DIAL*, WHICH WILL ALLOW HIM TO TRANSFORM FROM A 75-YEAR-OLD PROFESSOR INTO A REPLICA OF HIMSELF AT AGES 20, 30, 40, AND 50. THE WATCH, ALONG WITH A RANGE OF OTHER DEVICES AND THE HELP OF SEVERAL SUPERNATURAL CREATURES, ARE MEANT TO AID HIM IN HIS FIGHT FOR SOCIAL CHANGE.

AMONG DR. PALMER'S SUPERNATURAL ALLIES ARE THE *GUARDIAN GODS* OF ALL SEVEN CONTINENTS.

EUROPE, THE *GUARDIAN OF THE STARS,* CAN CAUSE THE STARS TO PROVIDE GUIDANCE AND DIRECTION FOR DR. PALMER!

ONE OF DR. PALMER'S DEVICES IS A *POWER SPEEDBOAT*, WHICH CAN REACH 150 MPH AND CONVERT INTO A SMALL CAR ON LAND!

GANGS

A GANG IS A GROUP OF PEOPLE WHO CLAIM A TERRITORY AND USE IT TO MAKE MONEY THROUGH ILLEGAL ACTIVITIES. GANGS CAN BE ORGANIZED BASED ON RACE, ETHNICITY, TERRITORY, OR MONEY-MAKING ACTIVITIES. THEIR MEMBERS ARE USUALLY YOUNG PEOPLE.

GANGS ARE VERY COMMON IN U.S. CITIES. IN FACT, 86% OF CITIES WITH A POPULATION OF 100,000 OR MORE REPORT GANG ACTIVITY.[13]

IN ADDITION, GANGS ARE ONE OF THE LEADING FACTORS FOR GROWTH OF VIOLENT CRIMES BOTH ON AND OFF SCHOOL PROPERTY.[14] GANG MEMBERS ARE ALSO MORE LIKELY TO BE ARRESTED OR INVOLVED WITH DRUGS AND ALCOHOL THAN NON-GANG MEMBERS.[15]

WHERE TO TURN?

WHERE SHOULD A YOUNG PERSON FACED WITH THIS ISSUE TURN? RESEARCH AND FILL OUT THE CONTACT INFORMATION BELOW.

IN YOUR CITY...
NAME: _____
PHONE: _____
EMAIL: _____

IN YOUR STATE...
NAME: _____
PHONE: _____
EMAIL: _____

IN YOUR COUNTY...
NAME: _____
PHONE: _____
EMAIL: _____

NATION-WIDE...
NAME: _____
PHONE: _____
EMAIL: _____

GENDER DISCRIMINATION

DR. PALMER, DISTINGUISHED PROFESSOR AND LIFELONG SOCIAL CHANGE ACTIVIST, ENCOUNTERS A MYSTERIOUS MAN CALLED MR. JAMES. UNKNOWN TO DR. PALMER, MR. JAMES IS AN *AGENT OF AGE.* PRIOR TO HIS DISAPPEARANCE, MR. JAMES LEAVES DR. PALMER HIS WRISTWATCH.

THE WATCH, DR. PALMER DISCOVERS, CONTAINS A HIDDEN *POWER DIAL,* WHICH WILL ALLOW HIM TO TRANSFORM FROM A 75-YEAR-OLD PROFESSOR INTO A REPLICA OF HIMSELF AT AGES 20, 30, 40, AND 50. THE WATCH, ALONG WITH A RANGE OF OTHER DEVICES AND THE HELP OF SEVERAL SUPERNATURAL CREATURES, ARE MEANT TO AID HIM IN HIS FIGHT FOR SOCIAL CHANGE.

AGENTS OF AGE, ARE THE *GUARDIANS OF THE LAWS OF TIME.* THEY ARE EACH ASSIGNED TO PROTECT AN ASPECT OF LIFE.

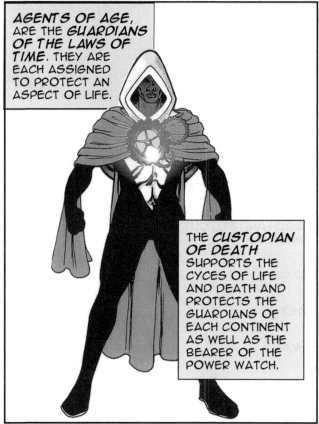

THE *CUSTODIAN OF DEATH* SUPPORTS THE CYCES OF LIFE AND DEATH AND PROTECTS THE GUARDIANS OF EACH CONTINENT AS WELL AS THE BEARER OF THE POWER WATCH.

AMONG DR. PALMER'S DEVICES IS A BULLETPROOF *POWER CAR* THAT CAN REACH UP TO 200 MPH AND FLOAT IN WATER!

GENDER DISCRIMINATION

GENDER DISCRIMINATION IS WHEN PEOPLE ARE TREATED UNFAIRLY COMPARED TO OTHERS BECAUSE OF THEIR GENDER.

GENDER DISCRIMINATION IS ESPECIALLY COMMON IN THE WORKPLACE. FOR INSTANCE, 42% OF WORKING WOMEN IN THE U.S. SAY THEY HAVE FACED DISCRIMINATION ON THE JOB BECAUSE OF THEIR GENDER.[16]

GENDER DISCRIMINATION IS ALSO RELATED TO UNEMPLOYMENT AND POVERTY. FOR EXAMPLE, TRANSGENDER AND GENDER NONCONFORMING PEOPLE EXPERIENCE UNEMPLOYMENT AT TWICE THE RATE AND EXTREME POVERTY AT FOUR TIMES THE RATE OF THE GENERAL POPULATION.[17]

WHERE TO TURN?

WHERE SHOULD A YOUNG PERSON FACED WITH THIS ISSUE TURN? RESEARCH AND FILL OUT THE CONTACT INFORMATION BELOW.

IN YOUR CITY...

NAME: _____

PHONE: _____

EMAIL: _____

IN YOUR STATE...

NAME: _____

PHONE: _____

EMAIL: _____

IN YOUR COUNTY...

NAME: _____

PHONE: _____

EMAIL: _____

NATION-WIDE...

NAME: _____

PHONE: _____

EMAIL: _____

COVID-19

DR. PALMER, DISTINGUISHED PROFESSOR AND LIFELONG SOCIAL CHANGE ACTIVIST, ENCOUNTERS A MYSTERIOUS MAN CALLED MR. JAMES. UNKNOWN TO DR. PALMER, MR. JAMES IS AN *AGENT OF AGE.* PRIOR TO HIS DISAPPEARANCE, MR. JAMES LEAVES DR. PALMER HIS WRISTWATCH.

THE WATCH, DR. PALMER DISCOVERS, CONTAINS A HIDDEN *POWER DIAL,* WHICH WILL ALLOW HIM TO TRANSFORM FROM A 75-YEAR-OLD PROFESSOR INTO A REPLICA OF HIMSELF AT AGES 20, 30, 40, AND SO. THE WATCH, ALONG WITH A RANGE OF OTHER DEVICES AND THE HELP OF SEVERAL SUPERNATURAL CREATURES, ARE MEANT TO AID HIM IN HIS FIGHT FOR SOCIAL CHANGE.

AGENTS OF AGE ARE THE *GUARDIANS OF THE LAWS OF TIME.* THEY ARE EACH ASSIGNED TO PROTECT AN ASPECT OF LIFE.

THE *CUSTODIAN OF LIFE* SUPPORTS ALL LIVING MATTER AND PROTECTS THE GUARDIANS OF EACH CONTINENT AS WELL AS THE BEARER OF THE POWER WATCH.

AMONG DR. PALMER'S DEVICES IS A *POWER JET PLANE* THAT CAN REACH 600-650 MPH AND CONVERT INTO A SMALL SUV ON LAND!

WHERE TO TURN?

WHERE SHOULD A YOUNG PERSON FACED WITH THIS ISSUE TURN? RESEARCH AND FILL OUT THE CONTACT INFORMATION BELOW.

IN YOUR CITY...

NAME: _____

PHONE: _____

EMAIL: _____

IN YOUR STATE...

NAME: _____

PHONE: _____

EMAIL: _____

IN YOUR COUNTY...

NAME: _____

PHONE: _____

EMAIL: _____

NATION-WIDE...

NAME: _____

PHONE: _____

EMAIL: _____

COVID-19

COVID-19 IS THE ILLNESS CAUSED BY A NEW CORONAVIRUS THAT SPREADS EASILY FROM PERSON TO PERSON.

YOU CAN BECOME INFECTED BY COMING INTO CLOSE CONTACT (WITHIN 6 FEET) OF A PERSON WHO HAS COVID-19. THE VIRUS SPREADS THROUGH RESPIRATORY DROPLETS WHEN AN INFECTED PERSON COUGHS, SNEEZES, OR TALKS. YOU MAY ALSO BECOME INFECTED BY TOUCHING A SURFACE OR OBJECT THAT HAS THE VIRUS ON IT, AND THEN TOUCHING YOUR MOUTH, NOSE, OR EYES.

IN ORDER TO PROTECT YOURSELF AND OTHERS FROM COVID-19, STAY AT HOME AS MUCH AS POSSIBLE AND AVOID CONTACT WITH OTHERS, WEAR A MASK IN PUBLIC SETTINGS, AND WASH YOUR HANDS FREQUENTLY.

Volume 2 Citations

1. National Council on Ageing. "Elder Abuse Facts." Accessed August 15, 2020, https://www.ncoa.org/public-policy-action/elder-justice/elder-abuse-facts/.

2. National Council on Ageing, "Elder Abuse Facts."

3. National Council on Ageing, "Elder Abuse Facts."

4. Renewable Resources Coalition. "Top 17 Environmental Problems." Accessed September 9, 2020, https://www.renewableresourcescoalition.org/top-environmental-problems/.

5. "Top 17 Environmental Problems."

6. Lopez, Mark Hugo et al. "Latinos and discrimination." *Pewresearch.org*, accessed August 12, 2020, https://www.pewresearch.org/hispanic/2018/10/25/latinos-and-discrimination/.

7. Child Trends. "Physical Fighting by Youth." Accessed August 19, 2020, https://www.childtrends.org/indicators/physical-fighting-by-youth.

8. "Physical Fighting by Youth."

9. Jacobson, G., et al. "Students Feeling Unsafe in School: Fifth Graders' Experiences." *The Journal of School Nursing* 27, no. 2 (2011): 149-159. http://www.ncbi.nlm.nih.gov/pmc/articles/PMC3103144/.

10. French, Laura. "9 facts about fire." *Firerescue1.org*, August 20, 2020. Accessed August 27, 2020, https://www.firerescue1.com/fire-products/firefighter-accountability/articles/9-facts-about-fire-CE8OwdOCiHdO7Unk/.

11. Addictions.com Medical Review. "10 Gambling Addiction Facts You Probably Don't Know." *Addictions.com*, October 25, 2018. Accessed August 27, 2020, https://www.addictions.com/gambling/10-gambling-addiction-facts-probably-dont-know/.

12. "10 Gambling Addiction Facts."

13. Carlie, Michael. "How to Join a Gang." *Into the Abyss: A Personal Journey into the World of Street Gangs*, accessed August 27, 2020, https://people.missouristate.edu/michaelcarlie/what_i_learned_about/gangs/join_a_gang.htm.

14. Grabianowski, Ed. "How Street Gangs Work." *Howstuffworks.com*, accessed August 27, 2020, https://people.howstuffworks.com/street-gang.htm.

15. Lebrun, Marcel. "Chapter Seven: Violence and Weapons." In *Children in Crisis: violence, victims, and victories*. Lanham, Md.: Rowman & Littlefield Education, 2011. 79-94.

16. Parker, Kim and Cary Funk. "Gender discrimination comes in many forms for today's working women." *Pewresearch.org*, December 14, 2017. Accessed August 19, 2020, https://www.pewresearch.org/fact-tank/2017/12/14/gender-discrimination-comes-in-many-forms-for-todays-working-women/.

17. Harrison, Jack et al. "A Gender Not Listed Here: Genderqueers, Gender Rebels, and OtherWise in the National Transgender Discrimination Survey." *LGBTQ Policy Journal at the Harvard Kennedy School*, Vol. 2, 2011-2012. Accessed August 19, 2020, http://www.thetaskforce.org/downloads/release_materials/agendernotlistedhere.pdf.

RESURRECTION
BLACK BOTTOM

Chapter 3

Volume 3 Table of Contents

GUN VIOLENCE

DR. PALMER, DISTINGUISHED PROFESSOR AND LIFELONG SOCIAL CHANGE ACTIVIST, ENCOUNTERS A MYSTERIOUS MAN CALLED MR. JAMES. UNKNOWN TO DR. PALMER, MR. JAMES IS AN *AGENT OF AGE*. PRIOR TO HIS DISAPPEARANCE, MR. JAMES LEAVES DR. PALMER HIS WRISTWATCH.

THE WATCH, DR. PALMER DISCOVERS, CONTAINS A HIDDEN *POWER DIAL*, WHICH WILL ALLOW HIM TO TRANSFORM FROM A 75-YEAR-OLD PROFESSOR INTO A REPLICA OF HIMSELF AT AGES 20, 30, 40, AND 50. THE WATCH, ALONG WITH A RANGE OF OTHER DEVICES AND THE HELP OF SEVERAL SUPERNATURAL CREATURES, ARE MEANT TO AID HIM IN HIS FIGHT FOR SOCIAL CHANGE.

AT AGE 20, DR. PALMER WAS AN *URBAN SURVIVALIST*, AN EXPERT AT NAVIGATING IN A TOUGH ENVIRONMENT AND LOOKING OUT FOR THOSE AROUND HIM.

NOW, HE USES THE POWER DIAL TO TRANFORM INTO HIS 20-YEAR-OLD SELF TO CONTINUE FIGHTING THE CHALLENGES HE CONFRONTED THEN.

POWER DIALS ARE THE SOURCE OF AN AGENT OF AGE'S ABILITIES. THEY ACT AS LINKS TO THE *GREATNESS OF TIME*.

DR. PALMER'S POWER DIAL ENABLES HIM TO *TRAVEL THROUGH TIME*. IT ALSO TELLS TIME ANYWHERE IN THE WORLD AND PROVIDES STATS ON ANY LOCAL ENVIRONMENT.

WHERE TO TURN?

WHERE SHOULD A YOUNG PERSON FACED WITH THIS ISSUE TURN? RESEARCH AND FILL OUT THE CONTACT INFORMATION BELOW.

IN YOUR CITY...

NAME: _____

PHONE: _____

EMAIL: _____

IN YOUR STATE...

NAME: _____

PHONE: _____

EMAIL: _____

IN YOUR COUNTY...

NAME: _____

PHONE: _____

EMAIL: _____

NATION-WIDE...

NAME: _____

PHONE: _____

EMAIL: _____

GUN VIOLENCE

EVERY YEAR, MORE THAN 30,000 PEOPLE IN THE U.S. DIE BECAUSE OF *GUN VIOLENCE*.[1] IN ADDITION, 44% OF AMERICANS SAY THEY PERSONALLY KNOW SOMEONE WHO HAS BEEN SHOT WITH A GUN, EITHER ACCIDENTALLY OR INTENTIONALLY.[2]

MANY VICTIMS OF GUN VIOLENCE ARE YOUNG PEOPLE. IN FACT, FIREARMS ARE THE LEADING CAUSE OF DEATH FOR AMERICAN CHILDREN AND TEENS.[3]

THE EFFECTS OF GUN VIOLENCE ALSO VARY BY RACE. BLACK MEN ARE DISPROPORTIONATELY AFFECTED BY GUN VIOLENCE, DOMESTIC SHOOTINGS DISPROPORTIONATELY KILL OR INJURE BLACK WOMEN, AND MOST MASS SHOOTING VICTIMS ARE BLACK.[4]

HATE CRIMES

DR. PALMER, DISTINGUISHED PROFESSOR AND LIFELONG SOCIAL CHANGE ACTIVIST, ENCOUNTERS A MYSTERIOUS MAN CALLED MR. JAMES. UNKNOWN TO DR. PALMER, MR. JAMES IS AN *AGENT OF AGE*. PRIOR TO HIS DISAPPEARANCE, MR. JAMES LEAVES DR. PALMER HIS WRISTWATCH.

THE WATCH, DR. PALMER DISCOVERS, CONTAINS A HIDDEN *POWER DIAL*, WHICH WILL ALLOW HIM TO TRANSFORM FROM A 75-YEAR-OLD PROFESSOR INTO A REPLICA OF HIMSELF AT AGES 20, 30, 40, AND 50. THE WATCH, ALONG WITH A RANGE OF OTHER DEVICES AND THE HELP OF SEVERAL SUPERNATURAL CREATURES, ARE MEANT TO AID HIM IN HIS FIGHT FOR SOCIAL CHANGE.

AT AGE 30, DR. PALMER WAS A *BLACK POWER ACTIVIST*, WORKING LOCALLY AND NATIONALLY TO DEMAND JUSTICE.

NOW, HE USES THE POWER DIAL TO TRANFORM INTO HIS 30-YEAR-OLD SELF SO THAT HE CAN CONTINUE FIGHTING RACISM, DISCRIMINATION, AND HATE CRIMES.

ONE OF DR. PALMER'S DEVICES IS A PAIR OF *POWER SUNGLASSES*, WHICH PROVIDE HIM WITH DISTANT DAY AND NIGHT VISION AND ALLOW HIM TO SEE THROUGH DARKNESS, WALLS, RAIN, SNOW, AND DUST STORMS!

WHERE TO TURN?

WHERE SHOULD A YOUNG PERSON FACED WITH THIS ISSUE TURN? RESEARCH AND FILL OUT THE CONTACT INFORMATION BELOW.

IN YOUR CITY...

NAME: _____

PHONE: _____

EMAIL: _____

IN YOUR STATE...

NAME: _____

PHONE: _____

EMAIL: _____

IN YOUR COUNTY...

NAME: _____

PHONE: _____

EMAIL: _____

NATION-WIDE...

NAME: _____

PHONE: _____

EMAIL: _____

HATE CRIMES

HATE CRIMES ARE CRIMES MOTIVATED BY PREJUDICE AND TARGETED TOWARDS PARTICULAR PEOPLE BECAUSE OF THEIR RACE, RELIGION, ETHNICITY, SEXUALITY, OR OTHER ASPECTS OF THEIR IDENTITIES.

IN THE U.S., THE MAJORITY OF REPORTED HATE CRIMES ARE MOTIVATED BY RACE, ETHNICITY, OR ANCESTRY BIAS, FOLLOWED BY RELIGION AND THEN SEXUAL ORIENTATION.[5]

MANY OF THE PEOPLE WHO COMMIT HATE CRIMES ARE TEENAGERS AND YOUNG ADULTS - IN FACT, HALF OF ALL HATE CRIMES IN THE U.S. ARE COMMITTED BY PEOPLE BETWEEN THE AGES OF 15 AND 24.[6]

DR. PALMER, DISTINGUISHED PROFESSOR AND LIFELONG SOCIAL CHANGE ACTIVIST, ENCOUNTERS A MYSTERIOUS MAN CALLED MR. JAMES. UNKNOWN TO DR. PALMER, MR. JAMES IS AN **AGENT OF AGE**. PRIOR TO HIS DISAPPEARANCE, MR. JAMES LEAVES DR. PALMER HIS WRISTWATCH.

THE WATCH, DR. PALMER DISCOVERS, CONTAINS A HIDDEN **POWER DIAL**, WHICH WILL ALLOW HIM TO TRANSFORM FROM A 75-YEAR-OLD PROFESSOR INTO A REPLICA OF HIMSELF AT AGES 20, 30, 40, AND 50. THE WATCH, ALONG WITH A RANGE OF OTHER DEVICES AND THE HELP OF SEVERAL SUPERNATURAL CREATURES, ARE MEANT TO AID HIM IN HIS FIGHT FOR SOCIAL CHANGE.

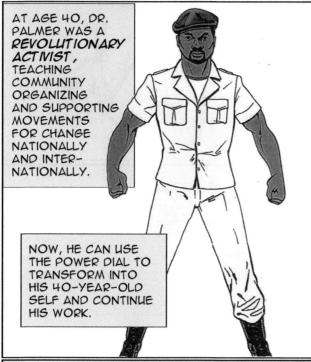

AT AGE 40, DR. PALMER WAS A **REVOLUTIONARY ACTIVIST**, TEACHING COMMUNITY ORGANIZING AND SUPPORTING MOVEMENTS FOR CHANGE NATIONALLY AND INTER-NATIONALLY.

NOW, HE CAN USE THE POWER DIAL TO TRANSFORM INTO HIS 40-YEAR-OLD SELF AND CONTINUE HIS WORK.

ONE OF DR. PALMER'S DEVICES IS A **POWER HEARING DEVICE**, WHICH CAN HEAR UP TO A MILE AWAY AND TRANSLATE ANY SPOKEN LANGUAGE INTO ENGLISH!

HIV/AIDS

HIV STANDS FOR HUMAN IMMUNODEFICIENCY VIRUS, AND **AIDS** STANDS FOR ACQUIRED IMMUNODEFICIENCY SYNDROME. AIDS IS THE MOST ADVANCED STAGE OF HIV, WHEN THE BODY'S IMMUNE SYSTEM IS HEAVILY WEAKENED.

HIV IS TRANSMITTED WHEN BODILY FLUIDS FROM AN INFECTED PERSON GET INTO THE BLOODSTREAM OF ANOTHER PERSON – FOR EXAMPLE, THROUGH UNPROTECTED SEX OR SHARING NEEDLES. HOWEVER, HIV CANNOT BE TRANSMITTED THROUGH SALIVA, SWEAT, SNEEZES, OR SKIN-TO-SKIN CONTACT.

ABOUT 1.1 MILLION PEOPLE IN THE U.S. ARE LIVING WITH HIV. AFRICAN AMERICANS ACCOUNTED FOR 43% OF NEW HIV DIAGNOSES IN 2017 AND 13% OF THE U.S. POPULATION.[7] LATINX PEOPLE ACCOUNTED FOR 26% OF NEW HIV DIAGNOSES AND 18% OF THE POPULATION.[8]

WHERE TO TURN?

WHERE SHOULD A YOUNG PERSON FACED WITH THIS ISSUE TURN? RESEARCH AND FILL OUT THE CONTACT INFORMATION BELOW.

IN YOUR CITY...
NAME: _____
PHONE: _____
EMAIL: _____

IN YOUR STATE...
NAME: _____
PHONE: _____
EMAIL: _____

IN YOUR COUNTY...
NAME: _____
PHONE: _____
EMAIL: _____

NATION-WIDE...
NAME: _____
PHONE: _____
EMAIL: _____

HOMELESSNESS

DR. PALMER, DISTINGUISHED PROFESSOR AND LIFELONG SOCIAL CHANGE ACTIVIST, ENCOUNTERS A MYSTERIOUS MAN CALLED MR. JAMES. UNKNOWN TO DR. PALMER, MR. JAMES IS AN *AGENT OF AGE.* PRIOR TO HIS DISAPPEARANCE, MR. JAMES LEAVES DR. PALMER HIS WRISTWATCH.

THE WATCH, DR. PALMER DISCOVERS, CONTAINS A HIDDEN *POWER DIAL,* WHICH WILL ALLOW HIM TO TRANSFORM FROM A 75-YEAR-OLD PROFESSOR INTO A REPLICA OF HIMSELF AT AGES 20, 30, 40, AND 50. THE WATCH, ALONG WITH A RANGE OF OTHER DEVICES AND THE HELP OF SEVERAL SUPERNATURAL CREATURES, ARE MEANT TO AID HIM IN HIS FIGHT FOR SOCIAL CHANGE.

AT AGE 50, DR. PALMER WAS AN *ACADEMIC ACTIVIST,* ADVOCATING ON BEHALF OF STUDENTS AND TEACHING REAL-WORLD LEADERSHIP SKILLS.

NOW, HE CAN USE THE POWER DIAL TO TRANFORM INTO HIS 50-YEAR-OLD SELF AND CONTINUE THIS WORK.

AMONG DR. PALMER'S DEVICES IS A *POWER BICYCLE,* WHICH HAS 12 SPEEDS AND CAN CLIMB HILLS AND MOUNTAINS!

WHERE TO TURN?

WHERE SHOULD A YOUNG PERSON FACED WITH THIS ISSUE TURN? RESEARCH AND FILL OUT THE CONTACT INFORMATION BELOW.

IN YOUR CITY...

NAME: _____

PHONE: _____

EMAIL: _____

IN YOUR STATE...

NAME: _____

PHONE: _____

EMAIL: _____

IN YOUR COUNTY...

NAME: _____

PHONE: _____

EMAIL: _____

NATION-WIDE...

NAME: _____

PHONE: _____

EMAIL: _____

HOMELESSNESS

ON ANY GIVEN NIGHT, MORE THAN 500,000 PEOPLE ARE EXPERIENCING *HOMELESSNESS* IN THE U.S.[9] IN ADDITION, ONE QUARTER OF HOMELESS PEOPLE ARE CHILDREN.[10]

MANY FACTORS CONTRIBUTE TO A PERSON BECOMING HOMELESS. AMONG WOMEN, DOMESTIC VIOLENCE IS A LEADING CAUSE OF HOMELESSNESS.[11] JOB LOSS, LACK OF HEALTHCARE, AND SUBSTANCE ABUSE ARE ALSO COMMON FACTORS.

CITIES ARE INCREASINGLY MAKING HOMELESSNESS A CRIME: MAKING IT ILLEGAL TO BEG IN PUBLIC, TO STAND AROUND OR LOITER, TO SLEEP ANYWHERE IN PUBLIC, OR TO SIT OR LIE DOWN IN SOME PUBLIC PLACES.

HOUSING DISCRIMINATION

DR. PALMER, DISTINGUISHED PROFESSOR AND LIFELONG SOCIAL CHANGE ACTIVIST, ENCOUNTERS A MYSTERIOUS MAN CALLED MR. JAMES. UNKNOWN TO DR. PALMER, MR. JAMES IS AN *AGENT OF AGE*. PRIOR TO HIS DISAPPEARANCE, MR. JAMES LEAVES DR. PALMER HIS WRISTWATCH.

THE WATCH, DR. PALMER DISCOVERS, CONTAINS A HIDDEN *POWER DIAL*, WHICH WILL ALLOW HIM TO TRANSFORM FROM A 75-YEAR-OLD PROFESSOR INTO A REPLICA OF HIMSELF AT AGES 20, 30, 40, AND 50. THE WATCH, ALONG WITH A RANGE OF OTHER DEVICES AND THE HELP OF SEVERAL SUPERNATURAL CREATURES, ARE MEANT TO AID HIM IN HIS FIGHT FOR SOCIAL CHANGE.

ONE OF DR. PALMER'S SUPERNATURAL ALLIES IS A GERMAN SHEPHERD GUARD DOG NAMED *WOLF*.

WOLF'S COLLAR CONTAINS A POWER DIAL SIMILAR TO THE ONE IN DR. PALMER'S WATCH. THE POWER DIAL GIVES WOLF SUPERNATURAL ABILITIES INCLUDING *IMMORTAL LIFE!*

AMONG DR. PALMER'S DEVICES IS A *POWER SONAR DEVICE*, WHICH ALLOWS HIM TO DETECT OBJECTS UNDERWATER!

WHERE TO TURN?

WHERE SHOULD A YOUNG PERSON FACED WITH THIS ISSUE TURN? RESEARCH AND FILL OUT THE CONTACT INFORMATION BELOW.

IN YOUR CITY...
NAME: _____
PHONE: _____
EMAIL: _____

IN YOUR STATE...
NAME: _____
PHONE: _____
EMAIL: _____

IN YOUR COUNTY...
NAME: _____
PHONE: _____
EMAIL: _____

NATION-WIDE...
NAME: _____
PHONE: _____
EMAIL: _____

HOUSING DISCRIMINATION

IT IS ESTIMATED THAT MORE THAN 4 MILLION CASES OF *HOUSING DISCRIMINATION* OCCUR EACH YEAR.[12]

OF COMPLAINTS MADE ABOUT DISCRIMINATION, OVER HALF ARE BASED ON ACCESSIBILITY BARRIERS AND OTHER DISABILITY-RELATED ISSUES, FOLLOWED BY THOSE BASED ON RACIAL DISCRIMINATION.[13]

MORE THAN 90% OF HOUSING DISCRIMINATION OCCURS AGAINST RENTERS, EVEN THOUGH RENTERS ARE OFTEN THOSE IN GREATER NEED OF AFFORDABLE HOUSING THAN HOMEOWNERS.[14]

HUMAN TRAFFICKING

DR. PALMER, DISTINGUISHED PROFESSOR AND LIFELONG SOCIAL CHANGE ACTIVIST, ENCOUNTERS A MYSTERIOUS MAN CALLED MR. JAMES. UNKNOWN TO DR. PALMER, MR. JAMES IS AN *AGENT OF AGE.* PRIOR TO HIS DISAPPEARANCE, MR. JAMES LEAVES DR. PALMER HIS WRISTWATCH.

THE WATCH, DR. PALMER DISCOVERS, CONTAINS A HIDDEN *POWER DIAL,* WHICH WILL ALLOW HIM TO TRANSFORM FROM A 75-YEAR-OLD PROFESSOR INTO A REPLICA OF HIMSELF AT AGES 20, 30, 40, AND 50. THE WATCH, ALONG WITH A RANGE OF OTHER DEVICES AND THE HELP OF SEVERAL SUPERNATURAL CREATURES, ARE MEANT TO AID HIM IN HIS FIGHT FOR SOCIAL CHANGE.

AMONG DR. PALMER'S SUPERNATURAL ALLIES ARE THE *GUARDIAN GODS* OF ALL SEVEN CONTINENTS.

NORTH AMERICA, THE *GUARDIAN OF WATER,* CAN CONTROL TIDES, BUILD GIANT WAVES, AND FLOOD RIVERS AND LAKES TO ASSIST DR. PALMER!

ONE OF DR. PALMER'S DEVICES IS A *POWER JET SKI,* WHICH CAN REACH 75-100 MPH AND CONVERT INTO A MOTORCYCLE ON LAND!

HUMAN TRAFFICKING

HUMAN TRAFFICKING IS WHEN PEOPLE ARE TRANSPORTED, BOUGHT AND SOLD IN SECRET. HUMAN TRAFFICKING HAPPENS EVERY YEAR, IN EVERY STATE IN THE U.S., AND BETWEEN COUNTRIES.

HUMAN TRAFFICKING TAKES MANY DIFFERENT FORMS, FROM SEX TRAFFICKING TO LABOR TRAFFICKING TO FORCED ORGAN REMOVAL TO FORCED MARRIAGE.

VICTIMS OF TRAFFICKING ARE OFTEN TRICKED AND THEN TRAPPED INTO A SITUATION THEY CAN'T ESCAPE. FOR INSTANCE, SOME ARE PROMISED A JOB AND A BETTER LIFE IN A FOREIGN COUNTRY AND THEN FORCED TO WORK FOR LITTLE OR NO PAY ONCE THEY ARRIVE.

WHERE TO TURN?

WHERE SHOULD A YOUNG PERSON FACED WITH THIS ISSUE TURN? RESEARCH AND FILL OUT THE CONTACT INFORMATION BELOW.

IN YOUR CITY...

NAME: _____

PHONE: _____

EMAIL: _____

IN YOUR STATE...

NAME: _____

PHONE: _____

EMAIL: _____

IN YOUR COUNTY...

NAME: _____

PHONE: _____

EMAIL: _____

NATION-WIDE...

NAME: _____

PHONE: _____

EMAIL: _____

HUNGER

DR. PALMER, DISTINGUISHED PROFESSOR AND LIFELONG SOCIAL CHANGE ACTIVIST, ENCOUNTERS A MYSTERIOUS MAN CALLED MR. JAMES. UNKNOWN TO DR. PALMER, MR. JAMES IS AN *AGENT OF AGE*. PRIOR TO HIS DISAPPEARANCE, MR. JAMES LEAVES DR. PALMER HIS WRISTWATCH.

THE WATCH, DR. PALMER DISCOVERS, CONTAINS A HIDDEN *POWER DIAL*, WHICH WILL ALLOW HIM TO TRANSFORM FROM A 75-YEAR-OLD PROFESSOR INTO A REPLICA OF HIMSELF AT AGES 20, 30, 40, AND 50. THE WATCH, ALONG WITH A RANGE OF OTHER DEVICES AND THE HELP OF SEVERAL SUPERNATURAL CREATURES, ARE MEANT TO AID HIM IN HIS FIGHT FOR SOCIAL CHANGE.

AMONG DR. PALMER'S SUPERNATURAL ALLIES ARE THE *GUARDIAN GODS* OF ALL SEVEN CONTINENTS.

AUSTRALIA, THE *GUARDIAN OF THE MOON*, CAN HAVE THE MOON RETREAT TO CAUSE DARKNESS, CONFUSION, AND A COVER FOR DR. PALMER!

ONE OF DR. PALMER'S DEVICES IS A *POWER RADAR DEVICE*, WHICH PROVIDES HIM WITH AIR SURVEILLANCE!

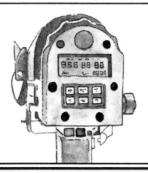

WHERE TO TURN?

WHERE SHOULD A YOUNG PERSON FACED WITH THIS ISSUE TURN? RESEARCH AND FILL OUT THE CONTACT INFORMATION BELOW.

IN YOUR CITY...

NAME: _____

PHONE: _____

EMAIL: _____

IN YOUR STATE...

NAME: _____

PHONE: _____

EMAIL: _____

IN YOUR COUNTY...

NAME: _____

PHONE: _____

EMAIL: _____

NATION-WIDE...

NAME: _____

PHONE: _____

EMAIL: _____

HUNGER

IN THE U.S., MORE THAN 37 MILLION PEOPLE STRUGGLE WITH HUNGER, INCLUDING MORE THAN 11 MILLION CHILDREN.[15] AROUND THE WORLD, NEARLY 1 BILLION PEOPLE DO NOT HAVE ENOUGH FOOD FOR A HEALTHY LIFE.[16]

HUNGER IS RELATED TO FOOD INSECURITY, WHICH IS WHEN A PERSON OR FAMILY HAS LIMITED OR UNCERTAIN ACCESS TO ENOUGH FOOD TO SUPPORT THEMSELVES.

POVERTY AND LACK OF RESOURCES AT INDIVIDUAL, LOCAL, AND NATIONAL LEVELS, AS WELL AS JOB INSTABILITY, FOOD SHORTAGES AND WASTE, UNSTABLE MARKETS, AND A RANGE OF OTHER FACTORS ALL CONTRIBUTE TO HUNGER.[17]

LABOR TRAFFICKING

DR. PALMER, DISTINGUISHED PROFESSOR AND LIFELONG SOCIAL CHANGE ACTIVIST, ENCOUNTERS A MYSTERIOUS MAN CALLED MR. JAMES. UNKNOWN TO DR. PALMER, MR. JAMES IS AN *AGENT OF AGE*. PRIOR TO HIS DISAPPEARANCE, MR. JAMES LEAVES DR. PALMER HIS WRISTWATCH.

THE WATCH, DR. PALMER DISCOVERS, CONTAINS A HIDDEN *POWER DIAL*, WHICH WILL ALLOW HIM TO TRANSFORM FROM A 75-YEAR-OLD PROFESSOR INTO A REPLICA OF HIMSELF AT AGES 20, 30, 40, AND 50. THE WATCH, ALONG WITH A RANGE OF OTHER DEVICES AND THE HELP OF SEVERAL SUPERNATURAL CREATURES, ARE MEANT TO AID HIM IN HIS FIGHT FOR SOCIAL CHANGE.

AMONG DR. PALMER'S SUPERNATURAL ALLIES ARE THE *GUARDIAN GODS* OF ALL SEVEN CONTINENTS.

THE ARCTIC, *GUARDIAN OF WIND*, CAN REDIRECT WIND, STORMS, HURRICANES, AND CYCLONES TO ASSIST DR. PALMER!

ONE OF DR. PALMER'S DEVICES IS A *POWER SUBMARINE*, A HYPER-SUBMARINE THAT CAN REACH SPEEDS OF UP TO 50 MPH UNDERWATER!

WHERE TO TURN?

WHERE SHOULD A YOUNG PERSON FACED WITH THIS ISSUE TURN? RESEARCH AND FILL OUT THE CONTACT INFORMATION BELOW.

IN YOUR CITY...

NAME: _____

PHONE: _____

EMAIL: _____

IN YOUR STATE...

NAME: _____

PHONE: _____

EMAIL: _____

IN YOUR COUNTY...

NAME: _____

PHONE: _____

EMAIL: _____

NATION-WIDE...

NAME: _____

PHONE: _____

EMAIL: _____

LABOR TRAFFICKING

LABOR TRAFFICKING IS A FORM OF HUMAN TRAFFICKING, OR MODERN-DAY SLAVERY. LABOR TRAFFICKING INCLUDES FORMS OF TRAFFICKING SUCH AS DEBT BONDAGE, FORCED LABOR, AND CHILD LABOR.

COMMON TYPES OF LABOR TRAFFICKING INCLUDE WHEN PEOPLE FORCED ARE TO WORK IN HOMES AS DOMESTIC SERVANTS, WHEN FARMWORKERS ARE COERCED THROUGH VIOLENCE AS THEY HARVEST CROPS, OR WHEN FACTORY WORKERS HELD IN INHUMANE CONDITIONS WITH LITTLE OR NO PAY.

LABOR TRAFFICKING VICTIMS MAKE A HIGH NUMBER OF CONSUMER GOODS AND FOOD PRODUCTS THAT ARE EITHER IMPORTED TO THE U.S. OR PRODUCED DOMESTICALLY. THE U.S. DEPARTMENT OF LABOR HAS IDENTIFIED 148 GOODS FROM 76 COUNTRIES THAT WERE MADE BY FORCED LABOR.[18]

LEAD POISONING

DR. PALMER, DISTINGUISHED PROFESSOR AND LIFELONG SOCIAL CHANGE ACTIVIST, ENCOUNTERS A MYSTERIOUS MAN CALLED MR. JAMES. UNKNOWN TO DR. PALMER, MR. JAMES IS AN *AGENT OF AGE.* PRIOR TO HIS DISAPPEARANCE, MR. JAMES LEAVES DR. PALMER HIS WRISTWATCH.

THE WATCH, DR. PALMER DISCOVERS, CONTAINS A HIDDEN *POWER DIAL,* WHICH WILL ALLOW HIM TO TRANSFORM FROM A 75-YEAR-OLD PROFESSOR INTO A REPLICA OF HIMSELF AT AGES 20, 30, 40, AND 50. THE WATCH, ALONG WITH A RANGE OF OTHER DEVICES AND THE HELP OF SEVERAL SUPERNATURAL CREATURES, ARE MEANT TO AID HIM IN HIS FIGHT FOR SOCIAL CHANGE.

AMONG DR. PALMER'S SUPERNATURAL ALLIES ARE THE *GUARDIAN GODS* OF ALL SEVEN CONTINENTS.

ASIA, THE *GUARDIAN OF THE SUN,* CAN ASSIST DR. PALMER BY INCREASING THE SUN'S HEAT OR CAUSING TEMPORARY BLINDNESS TO OVERWHELM AN ADVERSARY!

ONE OF DR. PALMER'S DEVICES IS A *POWER JETPACK,* WHICH CAN REACH SPEEDS OF 50 MPH AND TRAVEL AT UP TO 4000 FT ABOVE LAND!

LEAD POISONING

LEAD POISONING IS WHEN TOO MUCH LEAD ENTERS THE BODY FROM ACCIDENTALLY BREATHING, EATING, OR DRINKING IT.

LEAD IS TOXIC TO EVERYONE, BUT UNBORN BABIES AND YOUNG CHILDREN FACE THE GREATEST RISK BECAUSE THEIR BODIES ABSORB LEAD MORE EASILY THAN THOSE OF OLDER CHILDREN AND ADULTS.

THE MOST COMMON WAY THAT PEOPLE GET LEAD POISONING IS FROM LEAD-BASED PAINT, WHICH WAS USED ON MANY BUILDINGS BEFORE PEOPLE KNEW IT WAS HARMFUL. PEOPLE CAN ALSO GET LEAD POISONING FROM SOIL THAT HAS ABSORBED LEAD AND FROM WATER THAT FLOWS THROUGH OLD LEAD PIPES OR FAUCETS.

WHERE TO TURN?

WHERE SHOULD A YOUNG PERSON FACED WITH THIS ISSUE TURN? RESEARCH AND FILL OUT THE CONTACT INFORMATION BELOW.

IN YOUR CITY...
NAME: _____
PHONE: _____
EMAIL: _____

IN YOUR STATE...
NAME: _____
PHONE: _____
EMAIL: _____

IN YOUR COUNTY...
NAME: _____
PHONE: _____
EMAIL: _____

NATION-WIDE...
NAME: _____
PHONE: _____
EMAIL: _____

LGBT DISCRIMINATION

DR. PALMER, DISTINGUISHED PROFESSOR AND LIFELONG SOCIAL CHANGE ACTIVIST, ENCOUNTERS A MYSTERIOUS MAN CALLED MR. JAMES. UNKNOWN TO DR. PALMER, MR. JAMES IS AN *AGENT OF AGE*. PRIOR TO HIS DISAPPEARANCE, MR. JAMES LEAVES DR. PALMER HIS WRISTWATCH.

THE WATCH, DR. PALMER DISCOVERS, CONTAINS A HIDDEN *POWER DIAL*, WHICH WILL ALLOW HIM TO TRANSFORM FROM A 75-YEAR-OLD PROFESSOR INTO A REPLICA OF HIMSELF AT AGES 20, 30, 40, AND 50. THE WATCH, ALONG WITH A RANGE OF OTHER DEVICES AND THE HELP OF SEVERAL SUPERNATURAL CREATURES, ARE MEANT TO AID HIM IN HIS FIGHT FOR SOCIAL CHANGE.

AMONG DR. PALMER'S SUPERNATURAL ALLIES ARE THE *GUARDIAN GODS* OF ALL SEVEN CONTINENTS.

AFRICA, THE *GUARDIAN OF THE EARTH*, FIGHTS FOR PROTECTION OF THE ENVIRONMENT AND CAN AID DR. PALMER BY PROVIDING SHELTERS AND BLOCKADES OF EARTH!

ONE OF DR. PALMER'S DEVICES IS A *POWER MOTORCYCLE*, WHICH CAN REACH SPEEDS OF UP TO 150 MPH!

WHERE TO TURN?

WHERE SHOULD A YOUNG PERSON FACED WITH THIS ISSUE TURN? RESEARCH AND FILL OUT THE CONTACT INFORMATION BELOW.

IN YOUR CITY...

NAME: _____

PHONE: _____

EMAIL: _____

IN YOUR STATE...

NAME: _____

PHONE: _____

EMAIL: _____

IN YOUR COUNTY...

NAME: _____

PHONE: _____

EMAIL: _____

NATION-WIDE...

NAME: _____

PHONE: _____

EMAIL: _____

LGBT DISCRIMINATION

LGBT DISCRIMINATION IS WHEN SOMEONE IS TREATED UNFAIRLY BASED ON THEIR SEXUAL ORIENTATION OR GENDER IDENTITY.

YOUNG PEOPLE ARE OFTEN VICTIMS OF LGBT DISCRIMINATION. FOR INSTANCE, 80% OF GAY AND LESBIAN YOUTH REPORT SEVERE SOCIAL ISOLATION,[19] AND 6 IN 10 LGBT STUDENTS REPORT FEELING UNSAFE AT SCHOOL BECAUSE OF THEIR SEXUAL ORIENTATION.[20]

AMONG ADULTS, LGBT DISCRIMINATION IN THE WORKPLACE IS ESPECIALLY COMMON. MANY LGBT ADULTS REPORT BEING FIRED, NOT BEING HIRED, OR BEING DENIED A PROMOTION BECAUSE OF THEIR SEXUAL ORIENTATION OR GENDER IDENTITY.

Volume 3 Citations

1. "Fatal Injury Reports." *Injury Prevention & Control: Data & Statistics WISQARS.* Accessed August 27, 2020, https://webappa.cdc.gov/sasweb/ncipc/mortrate.html.

2. Igielnik, Ruth, and Anna Brown. "Key Takeaways on Americans' Views of Guns and Gun Ownership." *Pew Research Center.* Accessed August 27, 2020. www.pewresearch.org/fact- tank/2017/06/22/key-takeaways-on-americans-views-of-guns-and-gun-ownership/.

3. "Fatal Injury Reports."

4. Amnesty International. "Gun Violence – Key Facts." Accessed August 27, 2020, https://www.amnesty.org/en/what-we-do/arms-control/gun-violence/.

5. FBI. "2018 Hate Crime Statistics Released." Accessed August 27, 2020, https://www.fbi.gov/news/stories/2018-hate-crime-statistics-released-111219.

6. National Crime Prevention Council. "Tolerance for Teens." Accessed August 27, 2020, http://archive.ncpc.org/topics/hate-crime/tolerance.html.

7. HIV.gov. "U.S. Statistics." Accessed August 27, 2020, https://www.hiv.gov/hiv- basics/overview/data-and-trends/statistics.

8. "U.S. Statistics."

9. Front Steps. "U.S. Homelessness Facts." Accessed August 27, 2020, https://www.frontsteps.org/u-s-homelessness-facts/.

10. "U.S. Homelessness Facts."

11. "U.S. Homelessness Facts."

12. Thomas, Kelsey E. "This is What Housing Discrimination in the U.S. Looks Like." *Nextcity.org,* April 20, 2017. Accessed August 19, 2020, https://nextcity.org/daily/entry/housing- discrimination-us-report.

13. Thomas, "Housing Discrimination."

14. Thomas, "Housing Discrimination."

15. Feeding America. "Facts about poverty and hunger in America." Accessed August 27, 2020, https://www.feedingamerica.org/hunger-in-america/facts.

16. World Vision. "5 global hunger facts you need to know." Accessed August 27, 2020, https://www.worldvision.org/hunger-news-stories/global-hunger-facts.

17. Bread for the World. "About Hunger." Accessed August 27, 2020, https://www.bread.org/what-causes-hunger.

18. National Human Trafficking Hotline. "Labor Trafficking." Accessed August 27, 2020, https://humantraffickinghotline.org/type-trafficking/labor-trafficking.

19. National Dropout Prevention Center/Network. "Gay and Lesbian Youth." Accessed August 27, 2020, http://dropoutprevention.org/resources/statistics/gay-and-lesbian-youth/.

20. Kosciw, Joseph, et al. "The 2011 National School Climate Survey: The Experiences of Lesbian, Gay, Bisexual and Transgender Youth in Our Nation's Schools." Accessed August 27, 2020, https://www.glsen.org/sites/default/files/2020-04/2011%20GLSEN%20National%20School%20Climate%20Survey.pdf.

DOC PALMER!

Chapter 4

Volume 4 Table of Contents

DR. PALMER, DISTINGUISHED PROFESSOR AND LIFELONG SOCIAL CHANGE ACTIVIST, ENCOUNTERS A MYSTERIOUS MAN CALLED MR. JAMES. UNKNOWN TO DR. PALMER, MR. JAMES IS AN **AGENT OF AGE.** PRIOR TO HIS DISAPPEARANCE, MR. JAMES LEAVES DR. PALMER HIS WRISTWATCH.

THE WATCH, DR. PALMER DISCOVERS, CONTAINS A HIDDEN **POWER DIAL,** WHICH WILL ALLOW HIM TO TRANSFORM FROM A 75-YEAR-OLD PROFESSOR INTO A REPLICA OF HIMSELF AT AGES 20, 30, 40, AND 50. THE WATCH, ALONG WITH A RANGE OF OTHER DEVICES AND THE HELP OF SEVERAL SUPERNATURAL CREATURES, ARE MEANT TO AID HIM IN HIS FIGHT FOR SOCIAL CHANGE.

AT AGE 20, DR. PALMER WAS AN **URBAN SURVIVALIST,** AN EXPERT AT NAVIGATING IN A TOUGH ENVIRONMENT AND LOOKING OUT FOR THOSE AROUND HIM.

NOW, HE USES THE POWER DIAL TO TRANFORM INTO HIS 20-YEAR-OLD SELF TO CONTINUE FIGHTING THE CHALLENGES HE CONFRONTED THEN.

POWER DIALS ARE THE SOURCE OF AN AGENT OF AGE'S ABILITIES. THEY ACT AS LINKS TO THE **GREATNESS OF TIME.**

DR. PALMER'S POWER DIAL ENABLES HIM TO **TRAVEL THROUGH TIME.** IT ALSO TELLS TIME ANYWHERE IN THE WORLD AND PROVIDES STATS ON ANY LOCAL ENVIRONMENT.

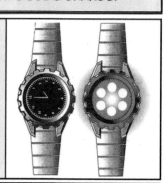

WHERE TO TURN?

WHERE SHOULD A YOUNG PERSON FACED WITH THIS ISSUE TURN? RESEARCH AND FILL OUT THE CONTACT INFORMATION BELOW.

IN YOUR CITY...

NAME: _____

PHONE: _____

EMAIL: _____

IN YOUR STATE...

NAME: _____

PHONE: _____

EMAIL: _____

IN YOUR COUNTY...

NAME: _____

PHONE: _____

EMAIL: _____

NATION-WIDE...

NAME: _____

PHONE: _____

EMAIL: _____

MENTAL HEALTH

IN THE U.S., MORE THAN 43 MILLION PEOPLE STRUGGLE WITH SOME FORM OF MENTAL ILLNESS.[1] AMONG THESE, ONE IN FIVE YOUNG PEOPLE AGED 13-18 LIVES WITH A MENTAL HEALTH CONDITION.[2]

MANY PEOPLE LACK ACCESS TO MENTAL HEALTH TREATMENT. IN FACT, OVER HALF OF ADULTS WITH A MENTAL ILLNESS DID NOT RECEIVE ANY CARE IN THE PAST YEAR.[3]

MANY FACTORS CONTRIBUTE TO A PERSON'S DEVELOPMENT OF A MENTAL HEALTH CONDITION, INCLUDING LIFE EXPERIENCES, BIOLOGICAL FACTORS, AND FAMILY HISTORY OF MENTAL ILLNESS.[4]

DR. PALMER, DISTINGUISHED PROFESSOR AND LIFELONG SOCIAL CHANGE ACTIVIST, ENCOUNTERS A MYSTERIOUS MAN CALLED MR. JAMES. UNKNOWN TO DR. PALMER, MR. JAMES IS AN *AGENT OF AGE.* PRIOR TO HIS DISAPPEARANCE, MR. JAMES LEAVES DR. PALMER HIS WRISTWATCH.

THE WATCH, DR. PALMER DISCOVERS, CONTAINS A HIDDEN *POWER DIAL,* WHICH WILL ALLOW HIM TO TRANSFORM FROM A 75-YEAR-OLD PROFESSOR INTO A REPLICA OF HIMSELF AT AGES 20, 30, 40, AND 50. THE WATCH, ALONG WITH A RANGE OF OTHER DEVICES AND THE HELP OF SEVERAL SUPERNATURAL CREATURES, ARE MEANT TO AID HIM IN HIS FIGHT FOR SOCIAL CHANGE.

AT AGE 30, DR. PALMER WAS A *BLACK POWER ACTIVIST,* WORKING LOCALLY AND NATIONALLY TO DEMAND JUSTICE.

NOW, HE USES THE POWER DIAL TO TRANFORM INTO HIS 30-YEAR-OLD SELF SO THAT HE CAN CONTINUE FIGHTING RACISM, DISCRIMINATION, AND HATE CRIMES.

ONE OF DR. PALMER'S DEVICES IS A PAIR OF *POWER SUNGLASSES,* WHICH PROVIDE HIM WITH DISTANT DAY AND NIGHT VISION AND ALLOW HIM TO SEE THROUGH DARKNESS, WALLS, RAIN, SNOW, AND DUST STORMS!

NUTRITION

NUTRITION IS AN IMPORTANT PART OF HEALTH AND DEVELOPMENT, ESPECIALLY AMONG YOUNG PEOPLE. THE BODY NEEDS CERTAIN NUTRIENTS, VITAMINS, AND MINERALS IN ORDER TO WORK ITS BEST. GOOD NUTRITION INVOLVES EATING A VARIETY OF FRUITS AND VEGETABLES, WHOLE GRAINS, AND A VARIETY OF PROTEIN FOODS.

HOWEVER, NUTRITION IS OFTEN A CHALLENGE DUE TO FACTORS INCLUDING LACK OF ACCESS TO HEALTHY FOODS. IN FACT, MORE THAN 23 MILLION AMERICANS, INCLUDING 6.5 MILLION CHILDREN, LIVE IN FOOD DESERTS - AREAS WHERE A SUPERMARKET IS NOT EASILY ACCESSIBLE.[5] IN ADDITION, MILLIONS OF PEOPLE FACE FOOD INSECURITY, OR LIMITED ACCESS TO NUTRITIONAL FOODS.[6]

WHERE TO TURN?

WHERE SHOULD A YOUNG PERSON FACED WITH THIS ISSUE TURN? RESEARCH AND FILL OUT THE CONTACT INFORMATION BELOW.

IN YOUR CITY...

NAME: _____

PHONE: _____

EMAIL: _____

IN YOUR STATE...

NAME: _____

PHONE: _____

EMAIL: _____

IN YOUR COUNTY...

NAME: _____

PHONE: _____

EMAIL: _____

NATION-WIDE...

NAME: _____

PHONE: _____

EMAIL: _____

OBESITY

DR. PALMER, DISTINGUISHED PROFESSOR AND LIFELONG SOCIAL CHANGE ACTIVIST, ENCOUNTERS A MYSTERIOUS MAN CALLED MR. JAMES. UNKNOWN TO DR. PALMER, MR. JAMES IS AN **AGENT OF AGE.** PRIOR TO HIS DISAPPEARANCE, MR. JAMES LEAVES DR. PALMER HIS WRISTWATCH.

THE WATCH, DR. PALMER DISCOVERS, CONTAINS A HIDDEN **POWER DIAL,** WHICH WILL ALLOW HIM TO TRANSFORM FROM A 75-YEAR-OLD PROFESSOR INTO A REPLICA OF HIMSELF AT AGES 20, 30, 40, AND 50. THE WATCH, ALONG WITH A RANGE OF OTHER DEVICES AND THE HELP OF SEVERAL SUPERNATURAL CREATURES, ARE MEANT TO AID HIM IN HIS FIGHT FOR SOCIAL CHANGE.

AT AGE 40, DR. PALMER WAS A **REVOLUTIONARY ACTIVIST,** TEACHING COMMUNITY ORGANIZING AND SUPPORTING MOVEMENTS FOR CHANGE NATIONALLY AND INTER-NATIONALLY.

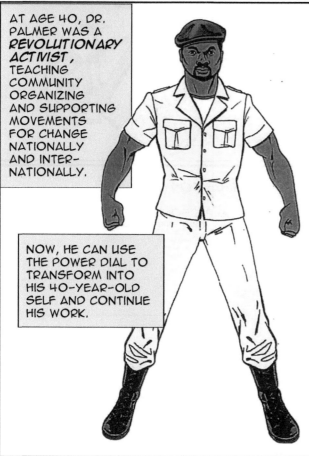

NOW, HE CAN USE THE POWER DIAL TO TRANSFORM INTO HIS 40-YEAR-OLD SELF AND CONTINUE HIS WORK.

ONE OF DR. PALMER'S DEVICES IS A **POWER HEARING DEVICE,** WHICH CAN HEAR UP TO A MILE AWAY AND TRANSLATE ANY SPOKEN LANGUAGE INTO ENGLISH!

WHERE TO TURN?

WHERE SHOULD A YOUNG PERSON FACED WITH THIS ISSUE TURN? RESEARCH AND FILL OUT THE CONTACT INFORMATION BELOW.

IN YOUR CITY...

NAME: _____

PHONE: _____

EMAIL: _____

IN YOUR STATE...

NAME: _____

PHONE: _____

EMAIL: _____

IN YOUR COUNTY...

NAME: _____

PHONE: _____

EMAIL: _____

NATION-WIDE...

NAME: _____

PHONE: _____

EMAIL: _____

OBESITY

OBESITY, OR WEIGHING SIGNIFICANTLY HIGHER THAN WHAT IS HEALTHY GIVEN ONE'S BODY MASS INDEX, IS A HEALTH CONDITION THAT ALSO INCREASES ONE'S RISK OF DEVELOPING PROBLEMS SUCH AS TYPE 2 DIABETES AND HIGH BLOOD PRESSURE.

OBESITY IS VERY COMMON IN THE U.S. – ABOUT 1 IN 5 KIDS AND TEENS[7] AND 2 IN 5 ADULTS[8] ARE OBESE. OBESITY IS CLOSELY RELATED TO NUTRITION AND LIFESTYLE. LACK OF ACCESS TO HEALTHY FOODS AND OPPORTUNITIES FOR EXERCISE ARE BOTH FACTORS THAT CONTRIBUTE TO OBESITY.

PEDOPHILIA

DR. PALMER, DISTINGUISHED PROFESSOR AND LIFELONG SOCIAL CHANGE ACTIVIST, ENCOUNTERS A MYSTERIOUS MAN CALLED MR. JAMES. UNKNOWN TO DR. PALMER, MR. JAMES IS AN *AGENT OF AGE*. PRIOR TO HIS DISAPPEARANCE, MR. JAMES LEAVES DR. PALMER HIS WRISTWATCH.

THE WATCH, DR. PALMER DISCOVERS, CONTAINS A HIDDEN *POWER DIAL*, WHICH WILL ALLOW HIM TO TRANSFORM FROM A 75-YEAR-OLD PROFESSOR INTO A REPLICA OF HIMSELF AT AGES 20, 30, 40, AND 50. THE WATCH, ALONG WITH A RANGE OF OTHER DEVICES AND THE HELP OF SEVERAL SUPERNATURAL CREATURES, ARE MEANT TO AID HIM IN HIS FIGHT FOR SOCIAL CHANGE.

AT AGE 50, DR. PALMER WAS AN *ACADEMIC ACTIVIST*, ADVOCATING ON BEHALF OF STUDENTS AND TEACHING REAL-WORLD LEADERSHIP SKILLS.

NOW, HE CAN USE THE POWER DIAL TO TRANFORM INTO HIS 50-YEAR-OLD SELF AND CONTINUE THIS WORK.

AMONG DR. PALMER'S DEVICES IS A *POWER BICYCLE*, WHICH HAS 12 SPEEDS AND CAN CLIMB HILLS AND MOUNTAINS!

WHERE TO TURN?

WHERE SHOULD A YOUNG PERSON FACED WITH THIS ISSUE TURN? RESEARCH AND FILL OUT THE CONTACT INFORMATION BELOW.

IN YOUR CITY...

NAME: _____

PHONE: _____

EMAIL: _____

IN YOUR STATE...

NAME: _____

PHONE: _____

EMAIL: _____

IN YOUR COUNTY...

NAME: _____

PHONE: _____

EMAIL: _____

NATION-WIDE...

NAME: _____

PHONE: _____

EMAIL: _____

PEDOPHILIA

PEDOPHILIA IS SEXUAL ABUSE OF CHILDREN BY ADULTS. PEDOPHILIA IS A WIDESPREAD FORM OF ABUSE – IN FACT, 1 IN 3 GIRLS AND 1 IN 5 BOYS ARE SEXUALLY ABUSED BEFORE THE AGE OF 18.[9] IN ADDITION, 90% OF CHILD SEXUAL ABUSE VICTIMS KNOW THE PERPETRATOR IN SOME WAY.[10]

PEDOPHILIA HAS LONG-TERM CONSEQUENCES. FOR INSTANCE, CHILD AND TEEN VICTIMS OF SEXUAL ABUSE ARE MORE LIKELY TO CONSIDER SUICIDE AS ADOLESCENTS THAN THOSE WHO HAVE NOT BEEN ABUSED.[11]

POISON

DR. PALMER, DISTINGUISHED PROFESSOR AND LIFELONG SOCIAL CHANGE ACTIVIST, ENCOUNTERS A MYSTERIOUS MAN CALLED MR. JAMES. UNKNOWN TO DR. PALMER, MR. JAMES IS AN *AGENT OF AGE*. PRIOR TO HIS DISAPPEARANCE, MR. JAMES LEAVES DR. PALMER HIS WRISTWATCH.

THE WATCH, DR. PALMER DISCOVERS, CONTAINS A HIDDEN *POWER DIAL*, WHICH WILL ALLOW HIM TO TRANSFORM FROM A 75-YEAR-OLD PROFESSOR INTO A REPLICA OF HIMSELF AT AGES 20, 30, 40, AND 50. THE WATCH, ALONG WITH A RANGE OF OTHER DEVICES AND THE HELP OF SEVERAL SUPERNATURAL CREATURES, ARE MEANT TO AID HIM IN HIS FIGHT FOR SOCIAL CHANGE.

ONE OF DR. PALMER'S SUPERNATURAL ALLIES IS A GERMAN SHEPHERD GUARD DOG NAMED *WOLF*.

WOLF'S COLLAR CONTAINS A POWER DIAL SIMILAR TO THE ONE IN DR. PALMER'S WATCH. THE POWER DIAL GIVES WOLF SUPERNATURAL ABILITIES INCLUDING *IMMORTAL LIFE!*

AMONG DR. PALMER'S DEVICES IS A *POWER SONAR DEVICE*, WHICH ALLOWS HIM TO DETECT OBJECTS UNDERWATER!

WHERE TO TURN?

WHERE SHOULD A YOUNG PERSON FACED WITH THIS ISSUE TURN? RESEARCH AND FILL OUT THE CONTACT INFORMATION BELOW.

IN YOUR CITY...

NAME: _____

PHONE: _____

EMAIL: _____

IN YOUR STATE...

NAME: _____

PHONE: _____

EMAIL: _____

IN YOUR COUNTY...

NAME: _____

PHONE: _____

EMAIL: _____

NATION-WIDE...

NAME: _____

PHONE: _____

EMAIL: _____

POISON

POISONING IS ONE OF THE MOST COMMON HEALTH EMERGENCIES FOR CHILDREN NATIONWIDE, AND IT IS THE FIFTH MOST COMMON CAUSE OF DEATH FROM INJURY.[19]

MANY POISONINGS OCCUR BECAUSE OF HOUSEHOLD PRODUCTS. LAWN, GARDEN, AND PESTICIDE CHEMICALS INTENDED TO CONTROL INSECTS, RODENTS, AND WEEDS ARE OFTEN AS TOXIC TO HUMANS AS THEY ARE TO THEIR INTENDED VICTIMS. FOOD POISONING CAN OCCUR FROM FOOD THAT'S STORED AT IMPROPER TEMPERATURES OR WHEN UTENSILS, COUNTERTOPS, STOVE TOPS, AND SINKS ARE NOT CLEANED.

POLICE ABUSE

DR. PALMER, DISTINGUISHED PROFESSOR AND LIFELONG SOCIAL CHANGE ACTIVIST, ENCOUNTERS A MYSTERIOUS MAN CALLED MR. JAMES. UNKNOWN TO DR. PALMER, MR. JAMES IS AN *AGENT OF AGE*. PRIOR TO HIS DISAPPEARANCE, MR. JAMES LEAVES DR. PALMER HIS WRISTWATCH.

THE WATCH, DR. PALMER DISCOVERS, CONTAINS A HIDDEN *POWER DIAL*, WHICH WILL ALLOW HIM TO TRANSFORM FROM A 75-YEAR-OLD PROFESSOR INTO A REPLICA OF HIMSELF AT AGES 20, 30, 40, AND 50. THE WATCH, ALONG WITH A RANGE OF OTHER DEVICES AND THE HELP OF SEVERAL SUPERNATURAL CREATURES, ARE MEANT TO AID HIM IN HIS FIGHT FOR SOCIAL CHANGE.

AGENTS OF AGE, ARE THE *GUARDIANS OF THE LAWS OF TIME*. THEY ARE EACH ASSIGNED TO PROTECT AN ASPECT OF LIFE.

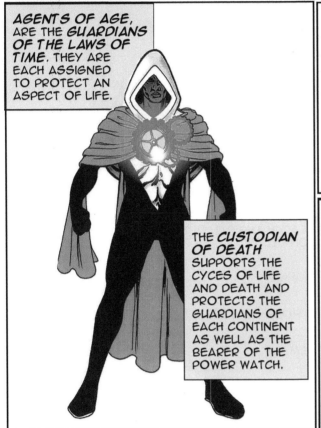

THE *CUSTODIAN OF DEATH* SUPPORTS THE CYCES OF LIFE AND DEATH AND PROTECTS THE GUARDIANS OF EACH CONTINENT AS WELL AS THE BEARER OF THE POWER WATCH.

AMONG DR. PALMER'S DEVICES IS A BULLETPROOF *POWER CAR* THAT CAN REACH UP TO 200 MPH AND FLOAT IN WATER!

WHERE TO TURN?

WHERE SHOULD A YOUNG PERSON FACED WITH THIS ISSUE TURN? RESEARCH AND FILL OUT THE CONTACT INFORMATION BELOW.

IN YOUR CITY...
NAME: _____
PHONE: _____
EMAIL: _____

IN YOUR STATE...
NAME: _____
PHONE: _____
EMAIL: _____

IN YOUR COUNTY...
NAME: _____
PHONE: _____
EMAIL: _____

NATION-WIDE...
NAME: _____
PHONE: _____
EMAIL: _____

POLICE ABUSE

POLICE ABUSE IS WHEN POLICE OFFICERS USE UNDUE OR EXCESSIVE FORCE AGAINST CIVILIANS. THIS RANGES FROM PHYSICAL AND VERBAL HARASSMENT TO PROPERTY DAMAGE TO INJURY OR DEATH.

WHILE POLICE KILL OVER 1,000 PEOPLE IN THE U.S. EACH YEAR, POLICE OFFICERS ARE CONVICTED IN ONLY 1% OF KILLINGS.[13]

IN ADDITION, THE GREATEST MAJORITY OF POLICE ABUSE VICTIMS ARE AFRICAN AMERICANS. IN FACT, AFRICAN AMERICAN PEOPLE ARE 3 TIMES MORE LIKELY TO BE KILLED BY A POLICE OFFICER THAN ARE WHITE PEOPLE.[14]

PUBLIC ACCOMMODATIONS DISCRIMINATION

DR. PALMER, DISTINGUISHED PROFESSOR AND LIFELONG SOCIAL CHANGE ACTIVIST, ENCOUNTERS A MYSTERIOUS MAN CALLED MR. JAMES. UNKNOWN TO DR. PALMER, MR. JAMES IS AN *AGENT OF AGE.* PRIOR TO HIS DISAPPEARANCE, MR. JAMES LEAVES DR. PALMER HIS WRISTWATCH.

THE WATCH, DR. PALMER DISCOVERS, CONTAINS A HIDDEN *POWER DIAL,* WHICH WILL ALLOW HIM TO TRANSFORM FROM A 75-YEAR-OLD PROFESSOR INTO A REPLICA OF HIMSELF AT AGES 20, 30, 40, AND 50. THE WATCH, ALONG WITH A RANGE OF OTHER DEVICES AND THE HELP OF SEVERAL SUPERNATURAL CREATURES, ARE MEANT TO AID HIM IN HIS FIGHT FOR SOCIAL CHANGE.

AGENTS OF AGE ARE THE *GUARDIANS OF THE LAWS OF TIME.* THEY ARE EACH ASSIGNED TO PROTECT AN ASPECT OF LIFE.

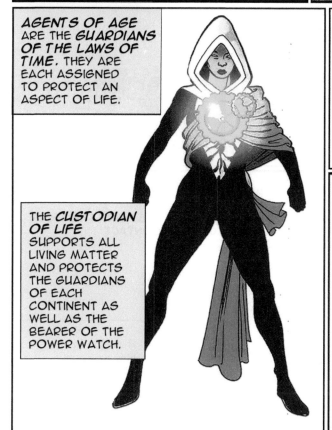

THE *CUSTODIAN OF LIFE* SUPPORTS ALL LIVING MATTER AND PROTECTS THE GUARDIANS OF EACH CONTINENT AS WELL AS THE BEARER OF THE POWER WATCH.

AMONG DR. PALMER'S DEVICES IS A *POWER JET PLANE* THAT CAN REACH 600-650 MPH AND CONVERT INTO A SMALL SUV ON LAND!

WHERE TO TURN?

WHERE SHOULD A YOUNG PERSON FACED WITH THIS ISSUE TURN? RESEARCH AND FILL OUT THE CONTACT INFORMATION BELOW.

IN YOUR CITY...

NAME: _____

PHONE: _____

EMAIL: _____

IN YOUR STATE...

NAME: _____

PHONE: _____

EMAIL: _____

IN YOUR COUNTY...

NAME: _____

PHONE: _____

EMAIL: _____

NATION-WIDE...

NAME: _____

PHONE: _____

EMAIL: _____

PUBLIC ACCOMMODATIONS DISCRIMINATION

PUBLIC ACCOMODATIONS DISCRIMINATION IS WHEN SOMEONE IS DENIED ACCESS TO THE FACILITIES OR SERVICES OF A BUSINESS OR OTHER PUBLIC PLACE. IT MAY HAPPEN WHEN SERVICES ARE DENIED OUTRIGHT, OR WHEN SOMEONE IS DENIED THE SAME SERVICES THAT OTHERS RECEIVE.

FOR EXAMPLE, IF A RESTAURANT OWNER REFUSES TO SERVE A CUSTOMER BECAUSE OF THEIR RACE, OR IF A GROCERY STORE REFUSES TO ALLOW FOR WHEELCHAIR ACCESSIBILITY, THIS IS PUBLIC ACCOMODATIONS DISCRIMINATION.

RACIAL DISCRIMINATION

DR. PALMER, DISTINGUISHED PROFESSOR AND LIFELONG SOCIAL CHANGE ACTIVIST, ENCOUNTERS A MYSTERIOUS MAN CALLED MR. JAMES. UNKNOWN TO DR. PALMER, MR. JAMES IS AN *AGENT OF AGE*. PRIOR TO HIS DISAPPEARANCE, MR. JAMES LEAVES DR. PALMER HIS WRISTWATCH.

THE WATCH, DR. PALMER DISCOVERS, CONTAINS A HIDDEN *POWER DIAL*, WHICH WILL ALLOW HIM TO TRANSFORM FROM A 75-YEAR-OLD PROFESSOR INTO A REPLICA OF HIMSELF AT AGES 20, 30, 40, AND 50. THE WATCH, ALONG WITH A RANGE OF OTHER DEVICES AND THE HELP OF SEVERAL SUPERNATURAL CREATURES, ARE MEANT TO AID HIM IN HIS FIGHT FOR SOCIAL CHANGE.

AMONG DR. PALMER'S SUPERNATURAL ALLIES ARE THE *GUARDIAN GODS* OF ALL SEVEN CONTINENTS.

THE ARCTIC, *GUARDIAN OF WIND*, CAN REDIRECT WIND, STORMS, HURRICANES, AND CYCLONES TO ASSIST DR. PALMER!

ONE OF DR. PALMER'S DEVICES IS A *POWER SUBMARINE*, A HYPER-SUBMARINE THAT CAN REACH SPEEDS OF UP TO 50 MPH UNDERWATER!

RACIAL DISCRIMINATION

RACIAL DISCRIMINATION IS WHEN SOMEONE IS TREATED UNFAIRLY BECAUSE OF THEIR RACE.

RACIAL DISCRIMINATION IS COMMON IN THE CRIMINAL LEGAL SYSTEM. THAT IS, BLACK AMERICANS ARE MORE LIKELY THAN WHITE AMERICANS TO BE ARRESTED, ONCE ARRESTED THEY ARE MORE LIKELY TO BE CONVICTED, AND ONCE CONVICTED THEY ARE MORE LIKELY TO RECEIVE LENGTHY PRISON SENTENCES.[15]

DISCRIMINATION ALSO OCCURS IN HEALTHCARE. FOR INSTANCE, FROM 2013-2017, WHITE PATIENTS IN THE U.S. RECEIVED BETTER QUALITY HEALTHCARE THAN ABOUT 34% OF HISPANIC PATIENTS, 40% OF BLACK PATIENTS, AND 40% OF NATIVE AMERICAN PATIENTS.[16]

DISCRIMINATION IS ALSO COMMON IN EMPLOYMENT. FOR EXAMPLE, IN THE U.S., BLACK PEOPLE ARE TWICE AS LIKELY TO BE UNEMPLOYED THAN WHITE PEOPLE. WHEN EMPLOYED, BLACK PEOPLE EARN NEARLY 25% LESS THAN WHITE PEOPLE.[17]

WHERE TO TURN?

WHERE SHOULD A YOUNG PERSON FACED WITH THIS ISSUE TURN? RESEARCH AND FILL OUT THE CONTACT INFORMATION BELOW.

IN YOUR CITY...

NAME: _____

PHONE: _____

EMAIL: _____

IN YOUR STATE...

NAME: _____

PHONE: _____

EMAIL: _____

IN YOUR COUNTY...

NAME: _____

PHONE: _____

EMAIL: _____

NATION-WIDE...

NAME: _____

PHONE: _____

EMAIL: _____

RELIGIOUS DISCRIMINATION

DR. PALMER, DISTINGUISHED PROFESSOR AND LIFELONG SOCIAL CHANGE ACTIVIST, ENCOUNTERS A MYSTERIOUS MAN CALLED MR. JAMES. UNKNOWN TO DR. PALMER, MR. JAMES IS AN *AGENT OF AGE.* PRIOR TO HIS DISAPPEARANCE, MR. JAMES LEAVES DR. PALMER HIS WRISTWATCH.

THE WATCH, DR. PALMER DISCOVERS, CONTAINS A HIDDEN *POWER DIAL,* WHICH WILL ALLOW HIM TO TRANSFORM FROM A 75-YEAR-OLD PROFESSOR INTO A REPLICA OF HIMSELF AT AGES 20, 30, 40, AND 50. THE WATCH, ALONG WITH A RANGE OF OTHER DEVICES AND THE HELP OF SEVERAL SUPERNATURAL CREATURES, ARE MEANT TO AID HIM IN HIS FIGHT FOR SOCIAL CHANGE.

AMONG DR. PALMER'S SUPERNATURAL ALLIES ARE THE *GUARDIAN GODS* OF ALL SEVEN CONTINENTS.

AUSTRALIA, THE *GUARDIAN OF THE MOON,* CAN HAVE THE MOON RETREAT TO CAUSE DARKNESS, CONFUSION, AND A COVER FOR DR. PALMER!

ONE OF DR. PALMER'S DEVICES IS A *POWER RADAR DEVICE,* WHICH PROVIDES HIM WITH AIR SURVEILLANCE!

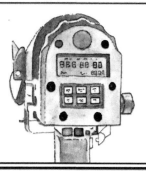

WHERE TO TURN?

WHERE SHOULD A YOUNG PERSON FACED WITH THIS ISSUE TURN? RESEARCH AND FILL OUT THE CONTACT INFORMATION BELOW.

IN YOUR CITY...

NAME: _____

PHONE: _____

EMAIL: _____

IN YOUR STATE...

NAME: _____

PHONE: _____

EMAIL: _____

IN YOUR COUNTY...

NAME: _____

PHONE: _____

EMAIL: _____

NATION-WIDE...

NAME: _____

PHONE: _____

EMAIL: _____

RELIGIOUS DISCRIMINATION

RELIGIOUS DISCRIMINATION IS WHEN SOMEONE IS TREATED UNEQUALLY BASED ON THEIR RELIGIOUS BELIEFS.

RELIGIOUS DISCRIMINATION ON AN INDIVIDUAL LEVEL CAN INCLUDE, FOR EXAMPLE, HARASSMENT OF WOMEN OVER RELIGIOUS DRESS OR HARASSMENT OF AN EMPLOYEE OR COWORKER BECAUSE OF THEIR RELIGION.

DISCRIMINATION ON A GOVERNMENTAL LEVEL CAN INCLUDE FAVORITISM OF A RELIGIOUS GROUP, LIMITS ON CONVERSION, PROHIBITION OF WORSHIP OR PRACTICE OF CERTAIN BELIEFS, OR VIOLENCE TOWARDS A MINORITY GROUP.

RUNAWAYS

DR. PALMER, DISTINGUISHED PROFESSOR AND LIFELONG SOCIAL CHANGE ACTIVIST, ENCOUNTERS A MYSTERIOUS MAN CALLED MR. JAMES. UNKNOWN TO DR. PALMER, MR. JAMES IS AN *AGENT OF AGE*. PRIOR TO HIS DISAPPEARANCE, MR. JAMES LEAVES DR. PALMER HIS WRISTWATCH.

THE WATCH, DR. PALMER DISCOVERS, CONTAINS A HIDDEN *POWER DIAL*, WHICH WILL ALLOW HIM TO TRANSFORM FROM A 75-YEAR-OLD PROFESSOR INTO A REPLICA OF HIMSELF AT AGES 20, 30, 40, AND 50. THE WATCH, ALONG WITH A RANGE OF OTHER DEVICES AND THE HELP OF SEVERAL SUPERNATURAL CREATURES, ARE MEANT TO AID HIM IN HIS FIGHT FOR SOCIAL CHANGE.

AMONG DR. PALMER'S SUPERNATURAL ALLIES ARE THE *GUARDIAN GODS* OF ALL SEVEN CONTINENTS.

ASIA, THE *GUARDIAN OF THE SUN,* CAN ASSIST DR. PALMER BY INCREASING THE SUN'S HEAT OR CAUSING TEMPORARY BLINDNESS TO OVERWHELM AN ADVERSARY!

ONE OF DR. PALMER'S DEVICES IS A *POWER JETPACK,* WHICH CAN REACH SPEEDS OF 50 MPH AND TRAVEL AT UP TO 4000 FT ABOVE LAND!

WHERE TO TURN?

WHERE SHOULD A YOUNG PERSON FACED WITH THIS ISSUE TURN? RESEARCH AND FILL OUT THE CONTACT INFORMATION BELOW.

IN YOUR CITY...

NAME: _____

PHONE: _____

EMAIL: _____

IN YOUR STATE...

NAME: _____

PHONE: _____

EMAIL: _____

IN YOUR COUNTY...

NAME: _____

PHONE: _____

EMAIL: _____

NATION-WIDE...

NAME: _____

PHONE: _____

EMAIL: _____

RUNAWAYS

RUNAWAYS ARE YOUNG PEOPLE WHO HAVE LEFT HOME WITHOUT THE PERMISSION OR KNOWLEDGE OF THEIR FAMILIES.

RUNNING AWAY FROM HOME IS ESPECIALLY COMMON AMONG TEENAGERS. IN FACT, BETWEEN 1.6 AND 2.8 MILLION TEENS RUN AWAY FROM HOME EACH YEAR.[18]

YOUNG PEOPLE USUALLY RUN AWAY DUE TO PROBLEMS AT HOME, PARTICULARLY ABUSE. IN ONE SURVEY, 80% OF YOUTH RUNAWAYS REPORTED THAT THEY HAD BEEN SEXUALLY OR PHYSICALLY ABUSED BEFORE RUNNING AWAY.[19]

HOWEVER, RUNNING AWAY FROM HOME PUTS YOUNG PEOPLE IN THE PATH OF NEW RISKS, SUCH AS BECOMING VICTIMS OF VIOLENCE OR TRAFFICKING.

Volume 4 Citations

1. Nguyen, Theresa, et al. "The State of Mental Health in America 2018." *Mental Health America,* accessed August 28, 2020, https://www.mhanational.org/issues/state-mental-health-america-2018.

2. Children's Health Council. "Mental Health Facts: Children and Teens." Accessed August 28, 2020, https://www.chconline.org/resourcelibrary/14183-2/.

3. Nguyen, "The State of Mental Health."

4. U.S. Department of Health and Human Services. "Mental Health Myths and Facts." Accessed August 28, 2020, https://www.mentalhealth.gov/basics/mental-health-myths-facts.

5. HHS.gov. "Facts and Statistics." Accessed December 19, 2020, https://www.hhs.gov/fitness/resource-center/facts-and-statistics/index.html.

6. HHS.gov, "Facts and Statistics."

7. CDC.gov. "Childhood Obesity Facts." Accessed August 28, 2020, https://www.cdc.gov/obesity/data/childhood.html.

8. CDC.gov. "Adult Obesity Facts." Accessed August 28, 2020, https://www.cdc.gov/obesity/data/adult.html.

9. Lauren's Kids. "Facts and Stats." Accessed August 28, 2020, https://laurenskids.org/awareness/about-faqs/facts-and-stats/.

10. Lauren's Kids, "Facts and Stats."

11. Lauren's Kids, "Facts and Stats."

12. City of Plantation. "Poisoning Facts." Accessed August 28, 2020, http://www.plantation.org/psd/Fire/text/fire-dept/lsf/poisoning.html.

13. Fact City. "9 Damaging Facts about Police Brutality." Accessed August 28, 2020, https://factcity.com/facts-about-police-brutality/.

14. "Police Brutality."

15. The Sentencing Project. "Report to the United Nations on Racial Disparities in the U.S. Criminal Justice System." Accessed September 11, 2020, https://www.sentencingproject.org/publications/un-report-on-racial-disparities/.

16. Agency for Healthcare Research and Quality. "National Healthcare Quality and Disparities Report." Accessed September 4, 2020, https://www.ahrq.gov/sites/default/files/wysiwyg/research/findings/nhqrdr/2018qdr-final.pdf.

17. Abdul Latif Jameel Poverty Action Lab. "Discrimination in the Job Market in the United States." Accessed September 4, 2020, https://www.povertyactionlab.org/evaluation/discrimination-job-market-united-states.

18. Hardy, Marcelina. "Teenage Runaway Facts." *Teens.lovetoknow.com,* accessed September 4, 2020, https://teens.lovetoknow.com/Teenage_Runaways.

19. Hardy, "Teenage Runaway Facts."

Chapter 5

Volume 5 Table of Contents

SCHOOL DROPOUT

 DR. PALMER, DISTINGUISHED PROFESSOR AND LIFELONG SOCIAL CHANGE ACTIVIST, ENCOUNTERS A MYSTERIOUS MAN CALLED MR. JAMES. UNKNOWN TO DR. PALMER, MR. JAMES IS AN **AGENT OF AGE**. PRIOR TO HIS DISAPPEARANCE, MR. JAMES LEAVES DR. PALMER HIS WRISTWATCH.

 THE WATCH, DR. PALMER DISCOVERS, CONTAINS A HIDDEN **POWER DIAL**, WHICH WILL ALLOW HIM TO TRANSFORM FROM A 75-YEAR-OLD PROFESSOR INTO A REPLICA OF HIMSELF AT AGES 20, 30, 40, AND 50. THE WATCH, ALONG WITH A RANGE OF OTHER DEVICES AND THE HELP OF SEVERAL SUPERNATURAL CREATURES, ARE MEANT TO AID HIM IN HIS FIGHT FOR SOCIAL CHANGE.

AT AGE 20, DR. PALMER WAS AN **URBAN SURVIVALIST**, AN EXPERT AT NAVIGATING IN A TOUGH ENVIRONMENT AND LOOKING OUT FOR THOSE AROUND HIM.

NOW, HE USES THE POWER DIAL TO TRANSFORM INTO HIS 20-YEAR-OLD SELF TO CONTINUE FIGHTING THE CHALLENGES HE CONFRONTED THEN.

POWER DIALS ARE THE SOURCE OF AN AGENT OF AGE'S ABILITIES. THEY ACT AS LINKS TO THE **GREATNESS OF TIME.**

DR. PALMER'S POWER DIAL ENABLES HIM TO **TRAVEL THROUGH TIME**. IT ALSO TELLS TIME ANYWHERE IN THE WORLD AND PROVIDES STATS ON ANY LOCAL ENVIRONMENT.

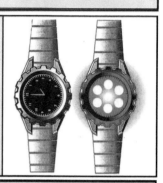

WHERE TO TURN?

WHERE SHOULD A YOUNG PERSON FACED WITH THIS ISSUE TURN? RESEARCH AND FILL OUT THE CONTACT INFORMATION BELOW.

IN YOUR CITY...

NAME: _____

PHONE: _____

EMAIL: _____

IN YOUR STATE...

NAME: _____

PHONE: _____

EMAIL: _____

IN YOUR COUNTY...

NAME: _____

PHONE: _____

EMAIL: _____

NATION-WIDE...

NAME: _____

PHONE: _____

EMAIL: _____

SCHOOL DROPOUT

SCHOOL DROPOUT IS WHEN STUDENTS LEAVE SCHOOL BEFORE GRADUATING. STUDENTS DROP OUT OF SCHOOL FOR MANY REASONS - FOR EXAMPLE, BECAUSE THEY ARE NOT ENGAGED IN WHAT THEY'RE LEARNING, BECAUSE THEY DON'T SEE SCHOOL AS RELEVANT TO THEIR LIVES, OR BECAUSE THEY FEEL PRESSURE TO EARN MONEY OR CARETAKE FOR A CHILD OR YOUNGER SIBLING.

SCHOOL DROPOUT RATES ARE VERY HIGH IN THE U.S. - ABOUT 25% OF FIRST-YEAR HIGH SCHOOL STUDENTS FAIL TO GRADUATE ON TIME.[1] IN ADDITION, THIS DROPOUT RATE VARIES BY RACE: BLACK AND HISPANIC STUDENTS ARE LESS LIKELY TO GRADUATE HIGH SCHOOL THAN ASIAN AND WHITE STUDENTS ARE.[2]

SEX TRAFFICKING

DR. PALMER, DISTINGUISHED PROFESSOR AND LIFELONG SOCIAL CHANGE ACTIVIST, ENCOUNTERS A MYSTERIOUS MAN CALLED MR. JAMES. UNKNOWN TO DR. PALMER, MR. JAMES IS AN *AGENT OF AGE.* PRIOR TO HIS DISAPPEARANCE, MR. JAMES LEAVES DR. PALMER HIS WRISTWATCH.

THE WATCH, DR. PALMER DISCOVERS, CONTAINS A HIDDEN *POWER DIAL,* WHICH WILL ALLOW HIM TO TRANSFORM FROM A 75-YEAR-OLD PROFESSOR INTO A REPLICA OF HIMSELF AT AGES 20, 30, 40, AND 50. THE WATCH, ALONG WITH A RANGE OF OTHER DEVICES AND THE HELP OF SEVERAL SUPERNATURAL CREATURES, ARE MEANT TO AID HIM IN HIS FIGHT FOR SOCIAL CHANGE.

AT AGE 30, DR. PALMER WAS A *BLACK POWER ACTIVIST,* WORKING LOCALLY AND NATIONALLY TO DEMAND JUSTICE.

NOW, HE USES THE POWER DIAL TO TRANFORM INTO HIS 30-YEAR-OLD SELF SO THAT HE CAN CONTINUE FIGHTING RACISM, DISCRIMINATION, AND HATE CRIMES.

ONE OF DR. PALMER'S DEVICES IS A PAIR OF *POWER SUNGLASSES,* WHICH PROVIDE HIM WITH DISTANT DAY AND NIGHT VISION AND ALLOW HIM TO SEE THROUGH DARKNESS, WALLS, RAIN, SNOW, AND DUST STORMS!

WHERE TO TURN?

WHERE SHOULD A YOUNG PERSON FACED WITH THIS ISSUE TURN? RESEARCH AND FILL OUT THE CONTACT INFORMATION BELOW.

IN YOUR CITY...
NAME: _____
PHONE: _____
EMAIL: _____

IN YOUR STATE...
NAME: _____
PHONE: _____
EMAIL: _____

IN YOUR COUNTY...
NAME: _____
PHONE: _____
EMAIL: _____

NATION-WIDE...
NAME: _____
PHONE: _____
EMAIL: _____

SEX TRAFFICKING

SEX TRAFFICKING IS HUMAN TRAFFICKING, OR MODERN-DAY SLAVERY, FOR THE PURPOSE OF SEXUAL EXPLOITATION.

HUMAN TRAFFICKING EARNS GLOBAL PROFITS OF ROUGHLY $150 BILLION A YEAR, $99 BILLION OF WHICH COMES FROM COMMERCIAL SEXUAL EXPLOITATION.[3]

IN 2018, OVER HALF OF THE HUMAN TRAFFICKING CASES ACTIVE IN THE U.S. WERE SEX TRAFFICKING CASES INVOLVING ONLY CHILDREN.[4] IN FACT, THE AVERAGE AGE A TEEN ENTERS THE SEX TRADE IS 12 TO 14 YEARS OLD. IN ADDITION, MANY OF THESE ARE RUNAWAY GIRLS WHO WERE SEXUALLY ABUSED AS CHILDREN.[5]

SEXUAL ASSAULT

DR. PALMER, DISTINGUISHED PROFESSOR AND LIFELONG SOCIAL CHANGE ACTIVIST, ENCOUNTERS A MYSTERIOUS MAN CALLED MR. JAMES. UNKNOWN TO DR. PALMER, MR. JAMES IS AN *AGENT OF AGE*. PRIOR TO HIS DISAPPEARANCE, MR. JAMES LEAVES DR. PALMER HIS WRISTWATCH.

THE WATCH, DR. PALMER DISCOVERS, CONTAINS A HIDDEN *POWER DIAL*, WHICH WILL ALLOW HIM TO TRANSFORM FROM A 75-YEAR-OLD PROFESSOR INTO A REPLICA OF HIMSELF AT AGES 20, 30, 40, AND 50. THE WATCH, ALONG WITH A RANGE OF OTHER DEVICES AND THE HELP OF SEVERAL SUPERNATURAL CREATURES, ARE MEANT TO AID HIM IN HIS FIGHT FOR SOCIAL CHANGE.

AT AGE 40, DR. PALMER WAS A *REVOLUTIONARY ACTIVIST*, TEACHING COMMUNITY ORGANIZING AND SUPPORTING MOVEMENTS FOR CHANGE NATIONALLY AND INTER-NATIONALLY.

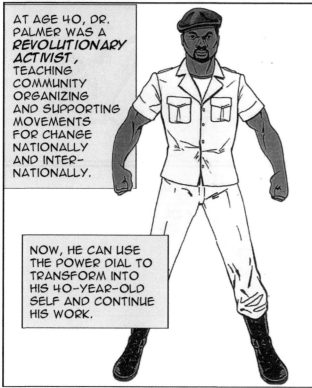

NOW, HE CAN USE THE POWER DIAL TO TRANSFORM INTO HIS 40-YEAR-OLD SELF AND CONTINUE HIS WORK.

ONE OF DR. PALMER'S DEVICES IS A *POWER HEARING DEVICE*, WHICH CAN HEAR UP TO A MILE AWAY AND TRANSLATE ANY SPOKEN LANGUAGE INTO ENGLISH!

WHERE TO TURN?

WHERE SHOULD A YOUNG PERSON FACED WITH THIS ISSUE TURN? RESEARCH AND FILL OUT THE CONTACT INFORMATION BELOW.

IN YOUR CITY...
NAME: _____
PHONE: _____
EMAIL: _____

IN YOUR STATE...
NAME: _____
PHONE: _____
EMAIL: _____

IN YOUR COUNTY...
NAME: _____
PHONE: _____
EMAIL: _____

NATION-WIDE...
NAME: _____
PHONE: _____
EMAIL: _____

SEXUAL ASSAULT

SEXUAL ASSAULT IS ANY NONCONSENSUAL SEXUAL ACT, INCLUDING WHEN SOMEONE DOES NOT HAVE THE ABILITY TO CONSENT.

SEXUAL ASSAULT IS ESPECIALLY COMMON ON COLLEGE CAMPUSES. IN FACT, NEARLY 1 IN 4 FEMALE COLLEGE STUDENTS EXPERIENCE SEXUAL ASSAULT.[6] IN ADDITION, IT IS ESTIMATED THAT ONLY A SMALL PERCENTAGE OF SEXUAL ASSAULTS ON COLLEGE CAMPUSES ARE REPORTED.[7]

THE CONSEQUENCES OF SEXUAL ASSAULT ARE FAR-REACHING. FOR INSTANCE, 4 OUT OF 5 RAPE VICTIMS SUFFER FROM CHRONIC PHYSICAL OR PSYCHOLOGICAL CONDITIONS.[8] IN ADDITION, RAPE SURVIVORS ARE MORE LIKELY TO ATTEMPT SUICIDE THAN ARE NON-SURVIVORS.[9]

SEXUAL HARASSMENT

DR. PALMER, DISTINGUISHED PROFESSOR AND LIFELONG SOCIAL CHANGE ACTIVIST, ENCOUNTERS A MYSTERIOUS MAN CALLED MR. JAMES. UNKNOWN TO DR. PALMER, MR. JAMES IS AN *AGENT OF AGE*. PRIOR TO HIS DISAPPEARANCE, MR. JAMES LEAVES DR. PALMER HIS WRISTWATCH.

THE WATCH, DR. PALMER DISCOVERS, CONTAINS A HIDDEN *POWER DIAL*, WHICH WILL ALLOW HIM TO TRANSFORM FROM A 75-YEAR-OLD PROFESSOR INTO A REPLICA OF HIMSELF AT AGES 20, 30, 40, AND 50. THE WATCH, ALONG WITH A RANGE OF OTHER DEVICES AND THE HELP OF SEVERAL SUPERNATURAL CREATURES, ARE MEANT TO AID HIM IN HIS FIGHT FOR SOCIAL CHANGE.

AT AGE 50, DR. PALMER WAS AN *ACADEMIC ACTIVIST*, ADVOCATING ON BEHALF OF STUDENTS AND TEACHING REAL-WORLD LEADERSHIP SKILLS.

NOW, HE CAN USE THE POWER DIAL TO TRANFORM INTO HIS 50-YEAR-OLD SELF AND CONTINUE THIS WORK.

AMONG DR. PALMER'S DEVICES IS A *POWER BICYCLE*, WHICH HAS 12 SPEEDS AND CAN CLIMB HILLS AND MOUNTAINS!

WHERE TO TURN?

WHERE SHOULD A YOUNG PERSON FACED WITH THIS ISSUE TURN? RESEARCH AND FILL OUT THE CONTACT INFORMATION BELOW.

IN YOUR CITY...

NAME: _____

PHONE: _____

EMAIL: _____

IN YOUR STATE...

NAME: _____

PHONE: _____

EMAIL: _____

IN YOUR COUNTY...

NAME: _____

PHONE: _____

EMAIL: _____

NATION-WIDE...

NAME: _____

PHONE: _____

EMAIL: _____

SEXUAL HARASSMENT

SEXUAL HARASSMENT INCLUDES COMMENTS, GESTURES, OR ACTIONS THAT ARE FOCUSED ON A PERSON'S APPEARANCE OR BODY PARTS AND ARE INTENDED TO HURT OR INTIMIDATE. SEXUAL HARASSMENT MAY BE VERBAL OR PHYSICAL, OR IT MIGHT TAKE THE FORM OF UNWANTED CALLS OR TEXTS.

SEXUAL HARASSMENT IS ESPECIALLY COMMON IN THE WORKPLACE. ONE REPORT FOUND THAT OVER HALF OF WORKING WOMEN HAD EXPERIENCED SOME FORM OF SEXUAL HARASSMENT AT THEIR JOBS.[10] IN ADDITION, FOR THOSE WHO REPORTED HARASSMENT, THE MAJORITY FOUND THAT NOTHING CHANGED AFTER THEY REPORTED IT; SOME EVEN SAID THAT THE SITUATION WORSENED.[11]

SPECIAL EDUCATION

DR. PALMER, DISTINGUISHED PROFESSOR AND LIFELONG SOCIAL CHANGE ACTIVIST, ENCOUNTERS A MYSTERIOUS MAN CALLED MR. JAMES. UNKNOWN TO DR. PALMER, MR. JAMES IS AN *AGENT OF AGE*. PRIOR TO HIS DISAPPEARANCE, MR. JAMES LEAVES DR. PALMER HIS WRISTWATCH.

THE WATCH, DR. PALMER DISCOVERS, CONTAINS A HIDDEN *POWER DIAL*, WHICH WILL ALLOW HIM TO TRANSFORM FROM A 75-YEAR-OLD PROFESSOR INTO A REPLICA OF HIMSELF AT AGES 20, 30, 40, AND 50. THE WATCH, ALONG WITH A RANGE OF OTHER DEVICES AND THE HELP OF SEVERAL SUPERNATURAL CREATURES, ARE MEANT TO AID HIM IN HIS FIGHT FOR SOCIAL CHANGE.

ONE OF DR. PALMER'S SUPERNATURAL ALLIES IS A GERMAN SHEPHERD GUARD DOG NAMED *WOLF*.

WOLF'S COLLAR CONTAINS A POWER DIAL SIMILAR TO THE ONE IN DR. PALMER'S WATCH. THE POWER DIAL GIVES WOLF SUPERNATURAL ABILITIES INCLUDING *IMMORTAL LIFE!*

AMONG DR. PALMER'S DEVICES IS A *POWER SONAR DEVICE*, WHICH ALLOWS HIM TO DETECT OBJECTS UNDERWATER!

WHERE TO TURN?

WHERE SHOULD A YOUNG PERSON FACED WITH THIS ISSUE TURN? RESEARCH AND FILL OUT THE CONTACT INFORMATION BELOW.

IN YOUR CITY...

NAME: _____

PHONE: _____

EMAIL: _____

IN YOUR STATE...

NAME: _____

PHONE: _____

EMAIL: _____

IN YOUR COUNTY...

NAME: _____

PHONE: _____

EMAIL: _____

NATION-WIDE...

NAME: _____

PHONE: _____

EMAIL: _____

SPECIAL EDUCATION

SPECIAL EDUCATION SERVES STUDENTS WITH MENTAL, PHYSICAL, EMOTIONAL, AND BEHAVIORAL DISABILITIES.

IN THE U.S., NEARLY 14% OF ALL STUDENTS AGED 13-21 ARE SPECIAL EDUCATION STUDENTS.[19] THE MAJORITY OF THESE STUDENTS, HOWEVER, SPEND MOST OF THEIR TIME IN REGULAR EDUCATION CLASSES.

SOME OF THE MOST COMMON LEARNING DISABILITIES INCLUDE *DYSLEXIA* (A DISORDER THAT AFFECTS ABILITY TO READ), *ADHD* (A DISORDER THAT AFFECTS ABILITY TO CONCENTRATE), *DYSCALCULA* (A DISORDER THAT AFFECTS ABILITIES WITH MATH), AND *DYSGRAPHIA* (A DISORDER THAT AFFECTS ABILITY TO WRITE).

STDS

DR. PALMER, DISTINGUISHED PROFESSOR AND LIFELONG SOCIAL CHANGE ACTIVIST, ENCOUNTERS A MYSTERIOUS MAN CALLED MR. JAMES. UNKNOWN TO DR. PALMER, MR. JAMES IS AN *AGENT OF AGE*. PRIOR TO HIS DISAPPEARANCE, MR. JAMES LEAVES DR. PALMER HIS WRISTWATCH.

THE WATCH, DR. PALMER DISCOVERS, CONTAINS A HIDDEN *POWER DIAL*, WHICH WILL ALLOW HIM TO TRANSFORM FROM A 75-YEAR-OLD PROFESSOR INTO A REPLICA OF HIMSELF AT AGES 20, 30, 40, AND 50. THE WATCH, ALONG WITH A RANGE OF OTHER DEVICES AND THE HELP OF SEVERAL SUPERNATURAL CREATURES, ARE MEANT TO AID HIM IN HIS FIGHT FOR SOCIAL CHANGE.

AMONG DR. PALMER'S SUPERNATURAL ALLIES ARE THE *GUARDIAN GODS* OF ALL SEVEN CONTINENTS.

THE ARCTIC, *GUARDIAN OF WIND*, CAN REDIRECT WIND, STORMS, HURRICANES, AND CYCLONES TO ASSIST DR. PALMER!

ONE OF DR. PALMER'S DEVICES IS A *POWER SUBMARINE*, A HYPER-SUBMARINE THAT CAN REACH SPEEDS OF UP TO 50 MPH UNDERWATER!

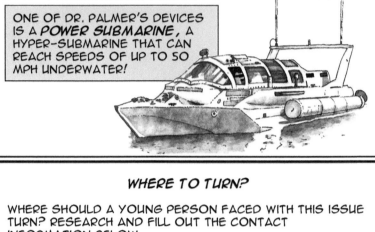

WHERE TO TURN?

WHERE SHOULD A YOUNG PERSON FACED WITH THIS ISSUE TURN? RESEARCH AND FILL OUT THE CONTACT INFORMATION BELOW.

IN YOUR CITY...

NAME: _____

PHONE: _____

EMAIL: _____

IN YOUR STATE...

NAME: _____

PHONE: _____

EMAIL: _____

IN YOUR COUNTY...

NAME: _____

PHONE: _____

EMAIL: _____

NATION-WIDE...

NAME: _____

PHONE: _____

EMAIL: _____

STDS

SEXUALLY TRANSMITTED DISEASES, OR *STDS*, ARE INFECTIONS THAT SPREAD FROM PERSON TO PERSON DURING SEX.

STDS ARE CAUSED BY BACTERIA, PARASITES, AND VIRUSES. ANTIBIOTICS CAN TREAT STDS CAUSED BY BACTERIA OR PARASITES. THERE IS NO CURE FOR STDS CAUSED BY A VIRUS, BUT MEDICINES CAN OFTEN HELP WITH THE SYMPTOMS.

MANY STDS HAVE NO SYMPTOMS OR ONLY MILD SYMPTOMS IN SOME PEOPLE, SO A PERSON CAN HAVE AND SPREAD STDS WITHOUT KNOWING. HOWEVER, LEFT UNTREATED MOST STDS LEAD TO SERIOUS HEALTH CONDITIONS OR EVEN DEATH.

STEALING

DR. PALMER, DISTINGUISHED PROFESSOR AND LIFELONG SOCIAL CHANGE ACTIVIST, ENCOUNTERS A MYSTERIOUS MAN CALLED MR. JAMES. UNKNOWN TO DR. PALMER, MR. JAMES IS AN *AGENT OF AGE*. PRIOR TO HIS DISAPPEARANCE, MR. JAMES LEAVES DR. PALMER HIS WRISTWATCH.

THE WATCH, DR. PALMER DISCOVERS, CONTAINS A HIDDEN *POWER DIAL*, WHICH WILL ALLOW HIM TO TRANSFORM FROM A 75-YEAR-OLD PROFESSOR INTO A REPLICA OF HIMSELF AT AGES 20, 30, 40, AND 50. THE WATCH, ALONG WITH A RANGE OF OTHER DEVICES AND THE HELP OF SEVERAL SUPERNATURAL CREATURES, ARE MEANT TO AID HIM IN HIS FIGHT FOR SOCIAL CHANGE.

AMONG DR. PALMER'S SUPERNATURAL ALLIES ARE THE *GUARDIAN GODS* OF ALL SEVEN CONTINENTS.

AFRICA, THE *GUARDIAN OF THE EARTH*, FIGHTS FOR PROTECTION OF THE ENVIRONMENT AND CAN AID DR. PALMER BY PROVIDING SHELTERS AND BLOCKADES OF EARTH!

ONE OF DR. PALMER'S DEVICES IS A *POWER MOTORCYCLE*, WHICH CAN REACH SPEEDS OF UP TO 150 MPH!

STEALING

STEALING IS TAKING SOMETHING THAT BELONGS TO SOMEONE ELSE WITHOUT THEIR PERMISSION. COMMON FORMS OF STEALING INCLUDE:

SHOPLIFTING: TAKING SOMETHING FROM A STORE WITHOUT PAYING.

BURGLARY: STEALING SOMETHING FROM SOMEONE'S HOME.

PLAGIARISM: TAKING SOMEONE ELSE'S WORDS OR IDEAS WITHOUT PERMISSION OR WITHOUT GIVING THEM CREDIT.

IDENTITY THEFT: USING ANOTHER PERSON'S NAME, BANK ACCOUNT, OR CREDIT CARD INFORMATION WITHOUT PERMISSION.

WHERE TO TURN?

WHERE SHOULD A YOUNG PERSON FACED WITH THIS ISSUE TURN? RESEARCH AND FILL OUT THE CONTACT INFORMATION BELOW.

IN YOUR CITY...

NAME: _____

PHONE: _____

EMAIL: _____

IN YOUR STATE...

NAME: _____

PHONE: _____

EMAIL: _____

IN YOUR COUNTY...

NAME: _____

PHONE: _____

EMAIL: _____

NATION-WIDE...

NAME: _____

PHONE: _____

EMAIL: _____

SUICIDE

DR. PALMER, DISTINGUISHED PROFESSOR AND LIFELONG SOCIAL CHANGE ACTIVIST, ENCOUNTERS A MYSTERIOUS MAN CALLED MR. JAMES. UNKNOWN TO DR. PALMER, MR. JAMES IS AN *AGENT OF AGE*. PRIOR TO HIS DISAPPEARANCE, MR. JAMES LEAVES DR. PALMER HIS WRISTWATCH.

THE WATCH, DR. PALMER DISCOVERS, CONTAINS A HIDDEN *POWER DIAL*, WHICH WILL ALLOW HIM TO TRANSFORM FROM A 75-YEAR-OLD PROFESSOR INTO A REPLICA OF HIMSELF AT AGES 20, 30, 40, AND SO. THE WATCH, ALONG WITH A RANGE OF OTHER DEVICES AND THE HELP OF SEVERAL SUPERNATURAL CREATURES, ARE MEANT TO AID HIM IN HIS FIGHT FOR SOCIAL CHANGE.

AMONG DR. PALMER'S SUPERNATURAL ALLIES ARE THE *GUARDIAN GODS* OF ALL SEVEN CONTINENTS.

EUROPE, THE *GUARDIAN OF THE STARS,* CAN CAUSE THE STARS TO PROVIDE GUIDANCE AND DIRECTION FOR DR. PALMER!

ONE OF DR. PALMER'S DEVICES IS A *POWER SPEEDBOAT,* WHICH CAN REACH 150 MPH AND CONVERT INTO A SMALL CAR ON LAND!

WHERE TO TURN?

WHERE SHOULD A YOUNG PERSON FACED WITH THIS ISSUE TURN? RESEARCH AND FILL OUT THE CONTACT INFORMATION BELOW.

IN YOUR CITY...

NAME: _____

PHONE: _____

EMAIL: _____

IN YOUR STATE...

NAME: _____

PHONE: _____

EMAIL: _____

IN YOUR COUNTY...

NAME: _____

PHONE: _____

EMAIL: _____

NATION-WIDE...

NAME: _____

PHONE: _____

EMAIL: _____

SUICIDE

SUICIDE IS ONE OF THE LEADING CAUSES OF DEATH AMONG CHILDREN, TEENAGERS, AND YOUNG ADULTS.[11]

PEOPLE WHO COMMIT SUICIDE ARE OFTEN SUFFERING FROM DEPRESSION, A DISORDER THAT INVOLVES EXTREME FEELINGS OF SADNESS AND HOPELESSNESS OVER A LONG PERIOD OF TIME. DEPRESSION CAN LEAD YOU TO BELIEVE THAT THINGS WILL NOT GET BETTER AND THAT LIFE IS NOT WORTH LIVING.

ESPECIALLY AMONG YOUNG PEOPLE, SUICIDE IS ALSO ASSOCIATED WITH FEELINGS OF STRESS, SELF-DOUBT, PRESSURE TO SUCCEED, FINANCIAL UNCERTAINTY, DISAPPOINTMENT, AND LOSS.[12]

TEEN PREGNANCY

DR. PALMER, DISTINGUISHED PROFESSOR AND LIFELONG SOCIAL CHANGE ACTIVIST, ENCOUNTERS A MYSTERIOUS MAN CALLED MR. JAMES. UNKNOWN TO DR. PALMER, MR. JAMES IS AN *AGENT OF AGE.* PRIOR TO HIS DISAPPEARANCE, MR. JAMES LEAVES DR. PALMER HIS WRISTWATCH.

THE WATCH, DR. PALMER DISCOVERS, CONTAINS A HIDDEN *POWER DIAL,* WHICH WILL ALLOW HIM TO TRANSFORM FROM A 75-YEAR-OLD PROFESSOR INTO A REPLICA OF HIMSELF AT AGES 20, 30, 40, AND 50. THE WATCH, ALONG WITH A RANGE OF OTHER DEVICES AND THE HELP OF SEVERAL SUPERNATURAL CREATURES, ARE MEANT TO AID HIM IN HIS FIGHT FOR SOCIAL CHANGE.

AMONG DR. PALMER'S SUPERNATURAL ALLIES ARE THE *GUARDIAN GODS* OF ALL SEVEN CONTINENTS.

ASIA, THE *GUARDIAN OF THE SUN,* CAN ASSIST DR. PALMER BY INCREASING THE SUN'S HEAT OR CAUSING TEMPORARY BLINDNESS TO OVERWHELM AN ADVERSARY!

ONE OF DR. PALMER'S DEVICES IS A *POWER JETPACK,* WHICH CAN REACH SPEEDS OF 50 MPH AND TRAVEL AT UP TO 4000 FT ABOVE LAND!

WHERE TO TURN?

WHERE SHOULD A YOUNG PERSON FACED WITH THIS ISSUE TURN? RESEARCH AND FILL OUT THE CONTACT INFORMATION BELOW.

IN YOUR CITY...

NAME: _____

PHONE: _____

EMAIL: _____

IN YOUR STATE...

NAME: _____

PHONE: _____

EMAIL: _____

IN YOUR COUNTY...

NAME: _____

PHONE: _____

EMAIL: _____

NATION-WIDE...

NAME: _____

PHONE: _____

EMAIL: _____

TEEN PREGNANCY

TEEN PREGNANCY IS VERY COMMON – IN FACT, IN THE U.S. 3 IN 10 GIRLS GET PREGNANT AT LEAST ONCE WHILE THEY ARE TEENAGERS.[15]

PREGNANCY AND BIRTH CONTRIBUTE TO HIGH SCHOOL DROPOUT RATES AMONG TEENAGE GIRLS. ONLY ABOUT 50% OF TEEN MOTHERS RECEIVE A HIGH SCHOOL DIPLOMA BY 22, WHEREAS ABOUT 90% OF WOMEN WHO DO NOT GIVE BIRTH AS TEENS GRADUATE FROM HIGH SCHOOL.[16]

TEEN PREGNANCY HAS CONSEQUENCES FOR CHILDREN BORN TO TEENS AS WELL: THEY ARE MORE LIKELY TO HAVE LOWER SCHOOL ACHIEVEMENT, TO GO TO PRISON AS TEENS, TO HAVE A CHILD AS A TEENAGER, AND TO FACE UNEMPLOYMENT AS A YOUNG ADULT.[17]

WATER SAFETY

DR. PALMER, DISTINGUISHED PROFESSOR AND LIFELONG SOCIAL CHANGE ACTIVIST, ENCOUNTERS A MYSTERIOUS MAN CALLED MR. JAMES. UNKNOWN TO DR. PALMER, MR. JAMES IS AN *AGENT OF AGE*. PRIOR TO HIS DISAPPEARANCE, MR. JAMES LEAVES DR. PALMER HIS WRISTWATCH.

THE WATCH, DR. PALMER DISCOVERS, CONTAINS A HIDDEN *POWER DIAL*, WHICH WILL ALLOW HIM TO TRANSFORM FROM A 75-YEAR-OLD PROFESSOR INTO A REPLICA OF HIMSELF AT AGES 20, 30, 40, AND 50. THE WATCH, ALONG WITH A RANGE OF OTHER DEVICES AND THE HELP OF SEVERAL SUPERNATURAL CREATURES, ARE MEANT TO AID HIM IN HIS FIGHT FOR SOCIAL CHANGE.

AMONG DR. PALMER'S SUPERNATURAL ALLIES ARE THE *GUARDIAN GODS* OF ALL SEVEN CONTINENTS.

NORTH AMERICA, THE *GUARDIAN OF WATER*, CAN CONTROL TIDES, BUILD GIANT WAVES, AND FLOOD RIVERS AND LAKES TO ASSIST DR. PALMER!

ONE OF DR. PALMER'S DEVICES IS A *POWER JET SKI*, WHICH CAN REACH 75-100 MPH AND CONVERT INTO A MOTORCYCLE ON LAND!

WHERE TO TURN?

WHERE SHOULD A YOUNG PERSON FACED WITH THIS ISSUE TURN? RESEARCH AND FILL OUT THE CONTACT INFORMATION BELOW.

IN YOUR CITY...

NAME: _____

PHONE: _____

EMAIL: _____

IN YOUR STATE...

NAME: _____

PHONE: _____

EMAIL: _____

IN YOUR COUNTY...

NAME: _____

PHONE: _____

EMAIL: _____

NATION-WIDE...

NAME: _____

PHONE: _____

EMAIL: _____

WATER SAFETY

WATER SAFETY INCLUDES THE PRECAUTIONS INTENDED TO MINIMIZE DANGER IN AND AROUND BODIES OF WATER.

WATER SAFETY IS IMPORTANT - IN FACT, DROWNING IS ONE OF THE MOST COMMON CAUSES OF ACCIDENTAL DEATH IN THE U.S.[18] DROWNING TAKES AN AVERAGE OF 3,500 TO 4,000 LIVES EVERY YEAR.[19] IN ADDITION, ABOUT 1 IN 5 PEOPLE WHO DIE FROM DROWNING ARE CHILDREN 14 AND YOUNGER.[20]

TAKING PRECAUTIONS MAKES A LARGE DIFFERENCE. FOR INSTANCE, LEARNING TO SWIM ALONE CAN REDUCE RISK OF DROWNING BY 88%.[21] EDUCATION ABOUT WATER SAFETY IS ALSO IMPORTANT IN PREVENTING DEATHS.

Volume 5 Citations

1. Silver, David, et al. "What Factors Predict High School Graduation in the Los Angeles Unified School District." *California Dropout Research Project* accessed September 4, 2020, https://www.issuelab.org/resources/11619/11619.pdf.

2. National Center for Education Statistics. "Trends in High School Dropout and Completion Rates in the United States: 2019." Accessed September 4, 2020, https://nces.ed.gov/pubs2020/2020117.pdf.

3. Human Rights First. "Human Trafficking by the Numbers." Accessed September 4, 2020, https://www.humanrightsfirst.org/resource/human-trafficking-numbers.

4. The Human Trafficking Institute. "2018 Federal Human Trafficking Report." Accessed September 4, 2020, https://www.traffickinginstitute.org/federal-human-trafficking-report-2018/.

5. Office of the Assistant Secretary for Planning and Evaluation. "Human Trafficking Into and Within the United States: A Review of the Literature." Accessed September 4, 2020, https://aspe.hhs.gov/report/human-trafficking-and-within-united-states-review-literature#Trafficking.

6. RAINN. "Campus Sexual Violence: Statistics." Accessed September 4, 2020, https://www.rainn.org/statistics/campus-sexual-violence.

7. AAUP. "Campus Sexual Assault: Suggested Policies and Procedures." Accessed September 4, 2020, http://www.aaup.org/report/campus-sexual-assault-suggested-policies-and-procedures.

8. National Criminal Justice Reference Service. "The Campus Sexual Assault Study." Accessed September 4, 2020, https://www.ncjrs.gov/pdffiles1/nij/grants/221153.pdf.

9. Networks for Life. "Identifying and Preventing Suicide in Post-Sexual Assault Care." Accessed September 4, 2020, https://www.wcsap.org/sites/default/files/uploads/webinars/Suicide_Intervention_Recording/Networks_for_Life_for_Sexual_Assault_Care.pdf.

10. Williams, Zoe. "Sexual harassment 101: what everyone needs to know." *The Guardian*, accessed September 4, 2020, https://www.theguardian.com/world/2017/oct/16/facts-sexual-harassment-workplace-harvey-weinstein.

11. Williams, "Sexual harassment 101."

12. Riser-Kositsky, Maya. "Special Education: Definition, Statistics, and Trends." *Education Week*, accessed September 4, 2020, https://www.edweek.org/ew/issues/special-populations/index.html.

13. AACAP. "Suicide in Children and Teens." Accessed September 4, 2020, https://www.aacap.org/AACAP/Families_and_Youth/Facts_for_Families/FFF-Guide/Teen-Suicide-010.aspx.

14. AACAP, "Suicide in Children and Teens."

15. Planned Parenthood. "Pregnancy and Childbearing Among U.S. Teens." Accessed September 4, 2020, https://www.plannedparenthood.org/files/5714/0545/7055/Pregnancy_And_Childbearing_Among_US_Teens.pdf.

16. Centers for Disease Control and Prevention. "About Teen Pregnancy." Accessed September 4, 2020, https://www.cdc.gov/teenpregnancy/about/index.htm.

17. Centers for Disease Control and Prevention, "About Teen Pregnancy."

18. National Drowning Prevention Alliance. "Water Safety Facts." Accessed September 4, 2020, https://ndpa.org/5-water-safety-facts/.

19. "Water Safety Facts."

20. "Water Safety Facts."

21. "Water Safety Facts."

A Brief Biography of Professor Walter Palmer

After a tumultuous juvenile life, Professor Palmer graduated from high school and was hired by the University of Pennsylvania hospital as a surgical attendant and eventually was recruited into the University of Pennsylvania School of Inhalation and Respiratory (Oxygen) Therapy.

After his certification as an inhalation and respiratory therapist, he was hired by the Children's Hospital of Philadelphia as the Director of the Department of Inhalation and Respiratory (Oxygen) Therapy, where he spent ten years helping to develop the national field of cardio-pulmonary therapy.

In 1955, Professor Palmer created the Palmer Foundation and the Black People's University of Philadelphia Freedom School and would spend the next seventy years developing leaders for social justice nationally.

Professor Palmer has also pursued further education at Temple University for Business Administration and Communications, Cheyney State University for a Teacher's Degree in History and Secondary Education. And at age 40, acquired his juris doctorate in law from Howard University.

Between 1965 and 1995, he produced and hosted radio programs on Philadelphia WDAS, Atlantic City WUSS, and WFPG Radio, in addition to Philadelphia NBC TV 10 and New Jersey Suburban Cable Television.

In 2006, he was inducted into the Philadelphia College of Physicians as a Fellow for the body of work he had done over the past 70 years, after having spent ten (1980-1990) years as a licensed financial officer teaching poor people how to overcome poverty by saving and investing three dollars per day.

During that entire period, Professor Palmer led the Civil Rights, Black Power and Afrocentric movements in Philadelphia, around the country as well as the Caribbean and West Indies.

In the 1980s to 2015, he led the school choice movement, organized a state-wide parental school choice group which collected 500,000 petitions in 1997, which were used to create a charter and cyber school law in Pennsylvania, and in 2000 the Walter D. Palmer School was named after him.

In 1962, he created a school without walls on the University of Pennsylvania's campus and became a visiting lecturer in the Schools of Medicine, Law, Education, Wharton, History, Africana Studies, Engineering, and he currently is a lecturer in the Schools of Medicine, Social Work, and Urban Studies, where he teaches courses on American racism.

In 1969, he helped the University of Pennsylvania Graduate School of Social Work students and faculty create required courses on American racism, making the University of Pennsylvania the first school in American academia to have such courses.

In 2019, Professor Palmer was appointed to the President's Commission on commemorating the four hundred year (1619) anniversary of American slavery.

Over his many years of teaching, he has received the title of Teacher Par Excellence and has amassed over 1,000 medals, trophies, plaques, certificates, and awards for participation in multiple disciplines.

Contributors

Akinseye Brown: Lead Artist
Akinseye Brown is a native Philadelphian and full-time illustrator who has worked on multiple freelance jobs and participated in a number of gallery exhibitions in the city. He is responsible for illustrating the W. D. Palmer characters.

Eric Battle: Supporting Artist
Eric Battle is a highly sought-after Philadelphia artist with an extensive portfolio of illustration work. He is responsible for the full-page Age of Justice poster.

Aaron Beatty: Supporting Artist
Aaron Beatty is a freelance artist and illustrator from Philadelphia. He is responsible for the Guardian illustrations for Africa, Asia, North and South America, the Artic, and Australia.

Walter D. Palmer: Story
Walter D. Palmer is responsible for creating the story and structure of the Age of Justice project.

Francesca Ciampa: Art Design and Layout
Francesca Ciampa is an undergraduate student at the University of Pennsylvania. She is responsible for layout and for illustrating the power devices and the Guardian character for Europe.

W.D. Palmer Foundation Publications

The Palmer Foundation was founded in 1955 and is a 501(c)3 tax-exempt organization that has spent over 65 years developing educational curriculum and learning materials for at-risk children, their parents, mentors, and teachers across the country.

We work with children from pre-school to high school with a focus on leadership, self-development, and social awareness.

Community Survivalist

Community Activist

International Activist

Human Rights Advocate

Contact Us

The W.D. Palmer Foundation (1955)
P.O. Box 22692
Philadelphia, PA 19110
(267) 738-1588
thewdpalmerfoundation@gmail.com
www.thewdpalmerfoundation.org
www.speakerservices.com

Donate to the W.D. Palmer Foundation

Make a donation (purchase), from the W.D. Palmer Foundation, a 501(c)3 tax-exempt organization that has worked for over 65 years to educate urban and rural "at-risk" children and their families, since 1955.

We have developed and published education curriculum and learning materials on leadership, self-development, and social awareness and how to overcome illiteracy, poverty, crime, and racism for urban and rural at-risk children and their families.

You will get a bulk discount for fifty (50) books or more, and the larger the order, the greater the discount. If you need less than fifty books, please order them directly from the publisher using the information below.

Order from us:
The W.D. Palmer Foundation
P.O. Box 22692
Philadelphia, PA 19110
www.thewdpalmerfoundation.org
wdpalmer@gmail.com
(267) 738-1588

Order from our publisher:
Author House
1663 Liberty Drive
Bloomington, IN 47403
www.authorhouse.com
(833) 262-8899

Part-time income
The W.D. Palmer Foundation is looking for community members and students that would like to earn extra income as independent sales representatives. Contact us to learn more.

Race and Racism

All Ebooks are $3.99+

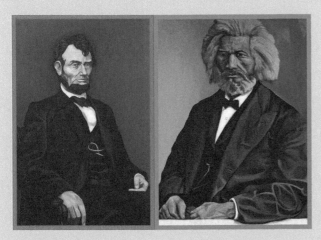

Everything You Must Know Before Race and Racism Dialogue

A precursor, dialogue, and debate about race and racism in America.

Where American Presidents Stood on Race and Racism in America

What position did each of the US presidents take on race and racism in America?

Race and Racism

All Ebooks are $3.99+

Racism in American Stage and Screen

How American stage and movies fostered racism in America and around the world.

Racism in America and Black Mental Health

How Black people were affected mentally by race and racism in America.

The W.D. Palmer Foundation
thewdpalmerfoundation@gmail.com thewdpalmerfoundation.org

History

All Ebooks are $3.99+

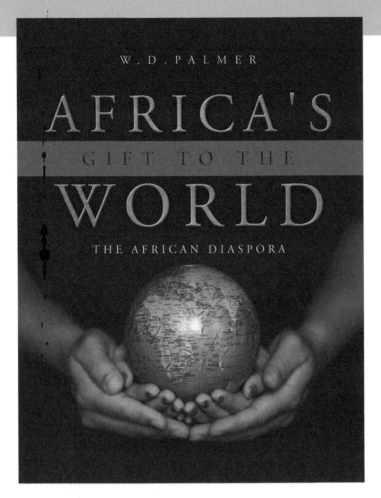

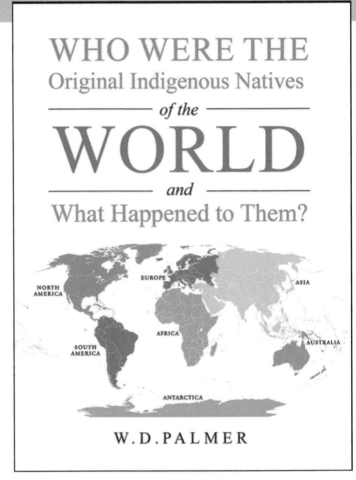

Africa's Gift to the World: The African Diaspora

How African humanity, culture, civilization, and history were spread all over the world through slavery.

Who were the Original Indigenous Natives of the World?

An attempt to answer questions of where people came from and where they went.

The W.D. Palmer Foundation
thewdpalmerfoundation@gmail.com thewdpalmerfoundation.org

Race, Racism, and Entertainment

All Ebooks are $3.99+

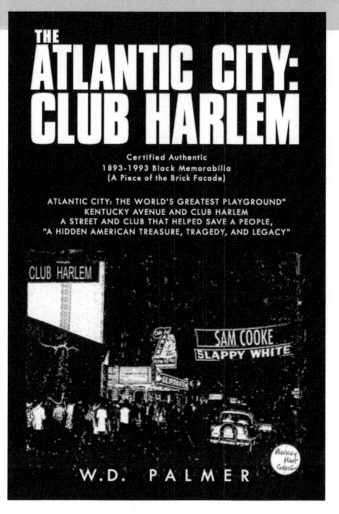

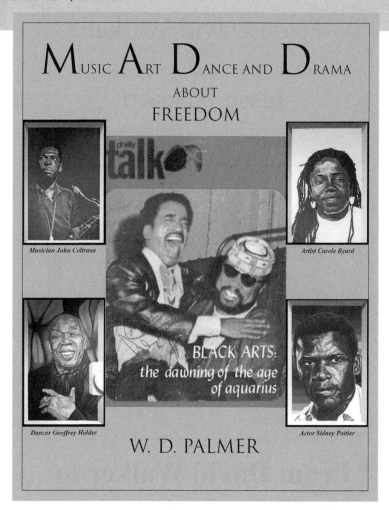

The Atlantic City Club Harlem
The story of how a nightclub was used to break down race and racism barriers in a small town.

MADD About Freedom
Major contributors in Music, Art, Dance, and Drama who used their talents for freedom.

The W.D. Palmer Foundation
thewdpalmerfoundation@gmail.com thewdpalmerfoundation.org

Leadership

All Ebooks are $3.99+

From David Walker
To
Jesse Jackson

David Walker
September 28 1796 - August 6, 1830

Jesse Jackson
October 8, 1941 - Present

Hollering for Freedom!

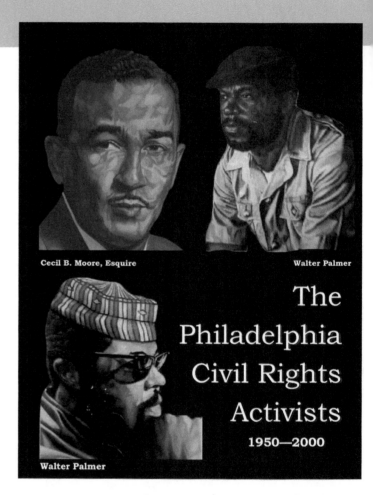

Cecil B. Moore, Esquire

Walter Palmer

The
Philadelphia
Civil Rights
Activists
1950—2000

Walter Palmer

From David Walker to Jesse Jackson

Some of the most vocal people who spoke out for freedom.

Philadelphia Civil Rights Activists: 1950-2000

How two men helped shape the history and destiny of a major metropolitan city.

The W.D. Palmer Foundation
thewdpalmerfoundation@gmail.com thewdpalmerfoundation.org

Youth Advocacy

All Ebooks are $3.99+

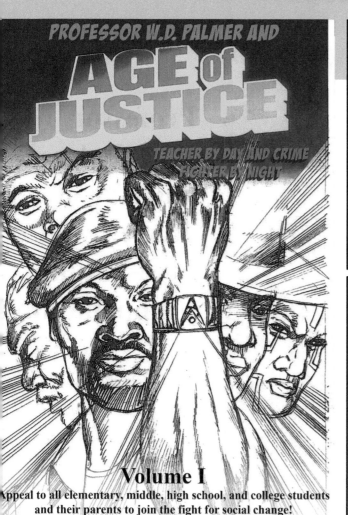

PROFESSOR W.D. PALMER AND

AGE of JUSTICE

TEACHER BY DAY AND CRIME FIGHTER BY NIGHT

Volume I

Appeal to all elementary, middle, high school, and college students and their parents to join the fight for social change!

Adopt an elementary, middle, high school, or college student, class, or school, or a church, for them to receive this survival guide

Volume I:
Alcohol Abuse
Animal Abuse
Asbestos
Bullying
Child Abuse
Disability
Disability Discrimination
Domestic Abuse
Drug Abuse
Education Discrimination

Volume II:
Elder Abuse
Employment Discrimination
Environmental Abuse
Ethnic Discrimination
Fighting
Fire Safety
Gambling Abuse
Gangs
Gender Discrimination
COVID-19

Volume III:
Gun Violence
Hate Crimes
HIV/AIDS
Homelessness
Housing Discrimination
Human Trafficking
Hunger
Labor Trafficking
Lead Poisoning
LGBT Discrimination

Volume IV:
Mental Health
Nutrition
Obesity
Pedophilia
Poison
Police Abuse
Public Accom. Discrim.
Racial Discrimination
Religious Discrimination
Runaways

Volume V:
School Dropout
Sex Trafficking
Sexual Assault
Sexual Harassment
Special Education
STDS
Stealing
Suicide
Teen Pregnancy
Water Safety

Professor W.D. Palmer and Age of Justice

A real-life comic hero appeal to parents, teachers, ministers, coaches, mentors, and monitors on how to help elementary, middle, high school, and first-year college students on where to turn in the face of danger.

The W.D. Palmer Foundation
thewdpalmerfoundation@gmail.com thewdpalmerfoundation.org

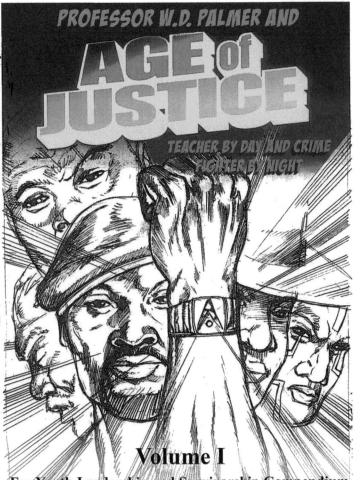

World Leaders

All Ebooks are $3.99+

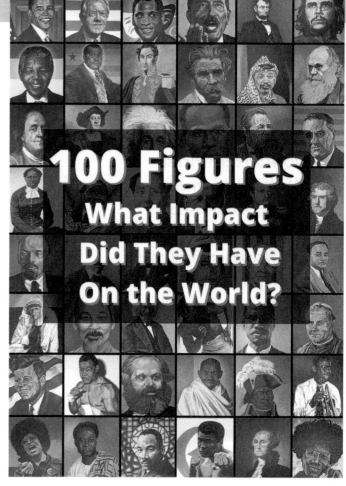

From Civil Rights Activists to Human Rights Advocates
How the fight for civil rights transformed activists into human rights advocates.

100 Figures
In what ways did 100 individuals impact the world?

W. D. Palmer Foundation Hashtags

1. #racedialogueusa
2. #racismdialogueusa
3. #atriskchildrenusa
4. #youthorganizingusa
5. #stopblackonblackusa
6. #newleadershipusa
7. #1619commemorationusa
8. #africanslaveryusa
9. #indigenouspeopleusa
10. #afrocentricusa
11. #civillibertiesusa
12. #civilrightsusa
13. #humanrightsusa
14. #saveourchildrenusa
15. #parentalschoolchoiceusa
16. #wearyourmaskusa
17. #defeatcovid19usa
18. #socialdistanceusa

91